THE NATURE OF OUR FATHER

EUGENE BAILEY

outskirtspress
DENVER, COLORADO

The Nature of Our Father
All Rights Reserved.
Copyright © 2013 Eugene Bailey
v1.0

Outskirts Press, Inc.
http://www.outskirtspress.com

ISBN: 978-1-4787-2050-8

Library of Congress Control Number: 2012946869

Outskirts Press and the "OP" logo are trademarks belonging to Outskirts Press, Inc.

PRINTED IN THE UNITED STATES OF AMERICA

Table of Contents

Introduction

There's a definite need in the world today for a clearer understanding of God's Word, a clearer understanding of who God is. It is not so much that the world needs a new Bible, for I believe that the truth of God's Word has always been with man. And never more has this truth been so evident than since Jesus, God's only begotten Son, came to earth to complete the finished work of His, and our, Father.

However, it is also my belief that the religious leaders from Jesus' times used God's Word as a means for power, wealth, and self-gain until the Word had become so diluted that it was almost unrecognizable, and without the Spirit of God to guide you, even today, you can be misled.

I am writing this book for one reason, and one reason only: that all people would come to know the nature of God through the understanding of His Word, and through the understanding of the finished work of Jesus. That people every-where, no matter what church building they go to or what religious name they go by, would come to call themselves children of God, first and foremost, above everything. And therefore, do what the Father would have them do ahead of what the leaders of a religious doctrine would have them believe is God's will.

If you will read this book with an open mind, an open heart, and an open Bible, you will learn the truth of who you are, the truth of what you will be-come, the truth of how everything came to be. And more important than these truths, you will learn who your Heavenly Father is, and what His nature is, so that no one—ever again—will be able to mislead you about who your God is, or why He did what He did.

And if I am successful, you will not only know of the love of your Father, but you will feel His love within every fiber of your being. You will use it as the light to light your way as you walk in love in this world. You will finally understand what your Father has always wanted for His creation—for His children—for you. You will understand what it means to be at peace, and at rest, and bask in the light that Jesus died to give us. You will learn that salvation is a gift from the Father, and that it requires nothing but belief for it to work in your life. You will also learn that salvation was not the only gift in the package brought to you by the sacrifice of Jesus.

1

In the Beginning

When trying to explain anything, I've always found it is easier if a person starts from the beginning. This fact does not change when trying to explain who we are, why we are here, and the nature of our Heavenly Father. Now in this case, the beginning is the start of man. And it's no coincidence that this is where the Bible starts.

In order to have a good clear understanding of anything, you must first believe in what is being presented to you. So for that purpose we must agree on a single fact that the Bible was given to us directly by God; that the Word of God is the absolute authority leading toward the understanding of His nature. If it cannot be proven by scripture, it is not His Word, and therefore, not His nature. And so we must first establish that the words written in the Bible were, and are, the ultimate guide to truth and knowledge, given to us by the Maker of all things.

John 1:3 states, "... and without Him nothing was made that was made," referring, of course, to God. Paul tells us when giving advice to his young protégé Timothy, that "All Scripture is given by inspiration of God, and is profitable for doctrine, for reproof, for correction, for instruction in righteousness, that the man of God may be complete, thoroughly equipped for every good work." (2 Timothy 3:16–17). We must believe that the intent and power given in His Word is as strong today as it ever was. That all the promises He made are still as valid and powerful as when He first made them. We must believe when it says in Isaiah 55:11, "So shall My word be that goes forth from My mouth; It shall not return to me void, But it shall accomplish what I please, and it shall prosper in the things for which I sent it."

God teaches man, as it says in Jeremiah 31:33–34, "But this is the covenant that I will make with the house of Israel after those days, says the Lord: I will put My law in their minds, and write it on their hearts; and I will be their God, and they shall be my people. No more shall every man teach his neighbor, and every man his brother, saying, 'Know the Lord,' for they all shall know Me, from the least of them to the greatest of them, says the Lord. For I will forgive their iniquity, and their sin I will remember no more."

And when scripture says in 1 Peter 1:23, "having been born again, not of corruptible seed but incorruptible, through the word of God which lives and abides forever," that the Word of God does, in fact, live and abide forever with man.

There may come a point while you are reading this book that you do not agree with the above because of the interpretation that you've been taught about a certain subject, because of a wrong doctrine. I would encourage you to go back to the ultimate filter for knowing and understanding the nature of God, His Word. And I would hope that you would see the same verses that you've seen so many times before, but in a new light. You will come to understand that some words that were used in the original translation of scripture were translated after man had already obtained a preconceived idea of God's Word, thus, changing the meaning, believing that the Word of God was only for the educated and the hierarchy of the world, which served man's purpose very well.

With the truth of the Word taken away from the common man, he could be more easily manipulated by religion. This misuse of the Word has helped to elevate the religious leaders throughout time to a place of power, through the ignorance of the masses. This is not the way the Father intended for His children to know Him. He sent His Son so that we might see His true nature, so that we might have a wonderful lasting relationship with Him because of the finished work of Jesus. He never wanted us to misunderstand about His love, or the fact that there is no longer any judgment by God. He wants us to learn about His love. He wants us to love Him and His children also with that same kind of love that Jesus demonstrated while He was living on the earth with man.

Now in the beginning there was nothing except God the Father and all that were with Him. We know that there was somebody with Him because in Genesis 1, God is clearly talking to someone, when He says in verse 26, "Let Us make man in Our image." You need to ask yourself who is with God even before man was formed from the dust. The answer is Jesus. He was there from the beginning.

Verse 26 goes on to say that God's intention was for this newly created man to be in charge of the newly created earth and everything on it. God goes on to bless and tells man to populate, and to have dominion over everything that moves in verse 28. So we are to understand in the beginning that man was given dominion over everything on the earth.

We understand that the nature of God is that of generosity and of the love of a Father toward His child. We understand that, up to this point, all the decisions made were perfect, because they were made by God.

There was only one problem in God's plan for man. He let man play a part in that plan. When God made man in His image, He also gave man free will, because God Himself has free will, and Jesus has free will. But with free will also came free choice.

You might ask yourself, if this was such a big problem, why did God give free will to man in the first place? The answer is very simple. Without free will and free choice we could have never been loved as sons of God. We could have never have gone to the Father with the kind of love that He wants from His children. We would have been something else that God created to fill the earth. But that was never what God intended for His children.

We must understand we were not created for the earth; the earth was created for us. But with free will, man had both the right and the obligation to make choices. And I am sorry to say that one of the first major choices of man recorded in the Bible would impact everything that man did for thousands of years.

When Adam made the choice to eat of the tree of knowledge, he made all that God the Father had planned for His children to be put on hold until God could correct this terrible mistake. We must understand that the law of God must also be obeyed by God, because He is God. So when the law was broken by Adam, God had no choice but to do what He did. It is plain to see that if Adam had made the right choice, there would not have been a need for the sacrifice of Jesus. But we must understand without a doubt that Adam made the worst decision that could possibly be made in this circumstance. And with that understanding of what Adam did comes the understanding of why Jesus had to do what He did.

We must realize that God's plan for man has never changed. What the Father wanted for His children then and what He wants for His children now are one and the same. God's nature has never changed since the beginning. He gave man a paradise to live in. He wanted man to be happy and content with everything that he did, thought, or felt. What we must realize in our hearts is that God still wants today what He wanted for His children back then. God's nature has never changed.

I think everyone knows the story about how the serpent came into the Garden and tempted Eve. And this story is absolutely true. But there are a couple of things I think that are pertinent to the understanding of who we are, who the Father is, and who we fight in this world. The adversary that was in the Garden is the same adversary, or enemy, that we have now. He has always been the enemy of God's children. And what is important about this is not that he has any strength, other than the strength that you give him. It is the fact of how he deceived Eve. He deceived her with a lie, but within the lie, there is enough truth to make it believable.

Your enemy will use the same trickery today that he used then. For instance, in Genesis 3:3, it says, "but of the fruit of the tree which is in the midst of the garden, God has said, 'You shall not eat it, nor shall you touch it, least you die.'" Verse 4–5 says, "Then the serpent said to the woman, 'You will not surely die. For God knows that in the day you eat of it your eyes will be opened, and you will be like God, knowing good and evil.'"

We know that their bodies did not die on that day. As a matter of fact, they went on to live a *very* long life. You might ask yourself the question, "Why is it that Adam didn't die?" The answer is something far worse than the death of the mortal body died that day: the innocence of man.

Before that day, Adam was as a child. And as a child, his mind and his heart were pure, without doubt, without fears. He never knew inadequacy or lack. Adam only knew love, kindness, fulfillment, and peace. But the most important thing that died on that day was the kind of relationship that Adam had with our Heavenly Father because now, he and every person with this new-found fear would run and hide from God, instead of seeking their Father out for a loving relationship.

How sad our Father must have been on that day. So when the adversary comes to you with a lie that you believe may have some truth in it, filter the lie with the knowledge of who your Father is and what His nature is toward His children because if Adam had trusted the Father, the adversary could not have used such a lie to deceive him. And if you trust the Father, you too can go unmolested by the adversary's lies.

It is true that on that day everything changed for man. But if you read the rest of Genesis 3, you will see that God, our Father, went to work immediately on the problem. But because it had to be corrected according to the law of God, it would take a little time, as we know time, for the law to be fulfilled. So we have learned our first lesson in knowing and understanding the nature of God.

First, God's plans have never changed from the beginning of creation until now. He still loves His children the same now as He did then. He still wants the same thing for them as He has always wanted. The relationship that was damaged by Adam in the Garden is now repaired and complete with the finished work of Jesus Christ.

Everything you judge, from the point of salvation forward, should be done while looking at the nature of your Father. If, when you look for God the Father, you don't see compassion, love, and forgiveness, then you're not looking to find the truth because you are filled with the idea that God wants to judge you, or that He is mad at you, that He has no forgiveness for you, or even worse, that He doesn't love you. If any of this wrong thinking should enter your heart, then you will do exactly like Adam did. You will run and hide because of the lies told to you by the enemy of God and man.

2

The Original Covenant

In Greek and Hebrew, the word "covenant" simply means, contract. To have a covenant was to have a common goal or cause, a contract, if you will, where two parties would agree on a certain outcome of the situation that was beneficial to both parties. Now when we look at the definition we can see that the covenant that God had with Adam was an agreement that was for the good of both God and man.

God made man and wanted to know him as a son, to have a relationship of love and understanding with him. He wanted to know him not just as something He had created, but to know that His child came to Him as a loving son. That he came to Him of his own free will. It was beneficial to man, because he was now in charge of a new world that God had made just for him, and all the benefits included therein. Man could now have all the love and protection of the Creator of that world.

In this original agreement, or contract, there was very little that man was not supposed to do in order for the contract to be upheld. But as we saw in the previous chapter, this was still too much responsibility for man to contend with for the contract to go unbroken. And after Adam had broken the covenant, or contract, between him and God, a new contract had to be established in order for God and man to retain their original relationship.

Many things happened on the day the original covenant was broken. But by far, the worst was that now there would be no more peace between man and God. There was still the love of the Father for His children. God has never stopped loving His children, nor will He ever stop loving His children. But the relationship between man and God changed for a very long time because when Adam broke this covenant, the law that was put into place by God had to be satisfied and obeyed.

The good news, however, was that our Father started immediately to repair the breach that man had caused, both in the agreement and also in man's relationship with Him. The first record of an animal's blood being spilled was right after God found out that Adam had broken the covenant. Genesis 3:21 states, "God made tunics of skin, and clothed them."

In Genesis 4:3–4, we find "And in the process of time it came to pass that Cain brought an offering of fruit of the ground to the Lord. Abel also brought of the firstborn of his flock and of their fat. And the Lord respected Abel and his offering." We must understand that now an offering of blood was required for the appeasement of the law. This was the only way to hold back judgment against man for the breach of the covenant. The covenant that was broken could not be repaired by the blood of animals. It could only be satisfied or appeased for a short time, until a permanent solution could be implemented by God.

But due to the lack of responsibility on man's part, we see that almost all of God's children were to perish. It says in Genesis 6:5–7, "Then the Lord saw that the wickedness of man was great in the earth, and that every intent of the thoughts of his heart was only evil continually. And the Lord was sorry that He had made man on the earth, and He was grieved in His heart."

Genesis 6:8, "But Noah found grace in the eyes of the Lord." This is significant because at that time, the world was completely corrupt, all of the time. God had no choice but to do away with it, but His grace was still alive, and His intention was still the same. He desired to have a relationship with His children. Verse 18 states, "But I will establish My covenant with you; and you shall go unto the ark—you, your sons, your wife, and your sons' wives with you."

We see in Genesis 8:20–21 that the first thing that Noah had to do when he exited the ark, after the rain had stopped and the water had subsided, was to appease the law with a sacrifice of blood from animals.

One of the most important parts in understanding the significance of the new covenant that we live in now is the understanding that God always knew how He would fix Adam's mistake. He always knew when He would fix Adam's mistake. And He made the information available to man about how He would correct the mistake. The breach in the law could only be corrected by a blood sacrifice. The only sacrifice sufficient to repair this monumental catechism was the blood of a sinless man. And now the reason becomes clear through the understanding of the sacrifice of our Lord and Savior Jesus Christ.

Genesis 17:7 tells us just that, "And I will establish My covenant between Me and you and your descendants after you in their generations, for an everlasting covenant, to be God to you and your descendants after you." The two things that are important in this verse are that, there will be a covenant, or a new contract, and that it will be one that will last forever. God the Father is telling Abraham that He has everything under control, that a plan is in place, that He knows how to rectify this problem so that it will be repaired forever.

We see later in the book of Exodus that man cried out to God to take His children and free them from the bondage of slavery. They indicated that now they wanted to have a relationship with their Father. And God, always having the same nature and the same goal for man, freed them. He gave them 613 laws to show them how they could appease sin and live a blessed life.

We must understand that all the sacrifices were only temporary, for the appeasement of the law, until the unblemished Lamb of God (Jesus) was ready to fulfill the law. But the most important thing was how man could have a relationship with Him. All throughout scripture we see that all that God the Father has ever wanted for His children was for them to have a loving relationship with Him. The important thing to realize here is that God never changed His mind about the covenant. He never quit believing in man no matter how many times man quit believing in Him. Our Father was determined that the covenant between Him and man would be fulfilled.

The book of Psalms, Proverbs, and especially Isaiah 53 and 54 illustrate how detailed the plans of God's new covenant would be. That everything that was lost with Adam and that original breach in the covenant would now be restored in full. That the peace that was lost between man and God would now be fully restored.

In Isaiah 54:9, God tells us that the new covenant of peace will be like the promise He made to the world after the flood. "For this is like the waters of Noah to Me; For as I have sworn that the waters of Noah would no longer cover the earth, so have I sworn that I would not be angry with you, nor rebuke you." So just as sure as the promise that God will never destroy the world with water again is the promise that He will never be angry with us again because of the new covenant. That once this breach between man and God was fixed that it will be fixed forever. Verse 10 says, "For the mountains shall depart and the hills be removed, but My kindness shall not depart from you, nor shall My covenant of peace be removed."

Therefore, we are to understand without the shadow of a doubt that after God finished His work through Jesus Christ, our Lord and Savior, that we will have peace with our Father until the end of time.

The questions that all of this pivot on are, did God our Father complete His work? Is God the Father true to His Word? And if He did repair everything with the new covenant, did the breach in the law stay fixed? To answer these three questions, we must remember that God cannot lie, so what He said in Isaiah so many years ago is as valid today as it was when He said it. He has finished the work of establishing a new covenant of peace through the death, burial, and resurrection of our Lord Jesus.

Hebrews 8:6 says that Jesus is a "Mediator of a better covenant, which was established on better promises." It goes on to say in verse 7 that "if that first covenant had been faultless, then no place would have been sought for a second."

Are you starting to realize by now that the flaw in the covenant between man and God was all the fault of man? If you will examine the new covenant of peace very carefully, you will see that man was given very little to do to make this contract between him and God work. You might say that God gave man a very small part in the new covenant of peace that we now live under. And for good reason man would have found a way to mess this covenant up also, if given half a chance. But because of man's limited participation in the covenant of peace, it has always been the perfect covenant to attain what the Father has always wanted for His children, and with His children.

Unfortunately, even with the limited participation of man, he still has managed to misconstrue the meaning of all that God the Father has done through this covenant, which has led to man being in bondage once again.

Most religion teaches only a part of the truth, of all that was given to us by the finished work of our Lord Jesus. Very few doctrines teach that we no longer live by the Law of Moses. They do not understand that if they will stop teaching the message of fear and judgment, and start teaching the message of love and forgiveness, that God's children could not hold back their urge to run to the Father for that wonderful relationship that awaits every one of His children.

Hebrews 1:2 tells us that through Jesus we now have that relationship with the Father. God "has in these days spoken to us by His Son." If the religious teachings of today would only convey the peace that comes with the new covenant, then the world would truly be at peace. Not because of anything that we did or could do, but because of the cross "and by Him to reconcile all things to Himself, by Him, whether things on earth or things in heaven, having made peace through the blood of His cross" (Colossians 1:20). So with this we understand that now there is peace on earth as well as in heaven. And if we can accept this fact, it will change everything we feel and do toward God our Father.

Philippians 4:7 states, "and the peace of God, which surpasses all understanding, will guard your hearts and minds through Christ Jesus." Why is it so important to guard your heart and your mind? As I wrote earlier in the chapter, the only way a man can mess up the new covenant was not to accept it as a fact. But when you accept all that Jesus did with your heart and mind, the peace of God, which the world will never understand, will become yours. The world does not understand the peace that a loving relationship with the Father brings to every one of His children if they are only willing to accept it.

You will only accept what you believe to be true. And what we believe with our minds will ultimately be written on our hearts. This is a very important part of how the world works. This will be covered more in-depth in a later chapter.

Religion and its doctrines are the problem with the acceptance of the covenant of peace. The church of today teaches that we still need the old covenant, or at least parts of it. They feel that if they don't impose some of the 613 Mosaic laws, that man will run wild, and if he goes unbridled, that sin will run rampant on the earth. That if man does not police himself, God's plan is incapable of working.

The church is afraid that with the acceptance of this wonderful revelation of peace between man and God, that mankind might establish a relationship with the Father, and therefore, there would be no need for the fear instigated by the church. And without that fear, what would possibly bring people to church? And if they don't bring the people to church, how will they get them to do the work of God without the guilt factor? And without guilt, how will we be able to extract 10 percent of man's income? And if they don't give their money, how will they live? Yes, the religious leaders of our time still use fear, judgment, and condemnation to control God's children, just as the religious leaders of Jesus' time used the same tactics to get rich and powerful.

Religion is under the misconception that this kind of tactic will bring people to the Father, when, in fact, we have a whole book called the Bible that says that way of thinking has never worked, and will never work.

Hebrews 7:18–19 explains it best: "For on the one hand there is an annulling of the former commandment because of its weakness and unprofitableness, for the law made nothing perfect [complete]; on the other hand, there is the bringing in of a better hope, through which we draw near to God." So by this, we are to understand two important facts. One, that because of man's inability to keep the law, the old covenant was weak and unprofitable. And because of the flaw, it made nothing for any man complete or perfect. Second, it has been annulled, or thrown away, for a better covenant that is perfect or complete. The new covenant will make God's children want to go to our Heavenly Father for a loving relationship.

The problem with the new covenant is it is too easy. History teaches us that man always takes something easy and makes it hard. Where would man be if all the people in the world understood that they don't need a man to teach them about God the Father? God said in Hebrews 8:11, "None of them shall teach his neighbor, and none his brother, saying, 'Know the Lord,' for all shall know Me, from the least of them to the greatest of them."

By receiving the spirit of God, you need no man to teach you who you are and who your Father is. That is why Jesus came to earth as a man, to teach us who the Heavenly Father is and what kind of a relationship we should have with Him. This also means that you shouldn't put any man higher than yourself when it comes to the love that the Father has for His children. He is no respecter of persons, and He loves all of his children equally.

If at any time a man or church or any religious organization tries to impose their laws or doctrines upon you, you should run—not walk—to the nearest exit. To live by anything but the new covenant is to live by something that is "obsolete and growing old ready to vanish away" (Hebrews 8:13).

The new covenant of peace is to be accepted as a contract. You do not need to understand how it works, just that it does work. The most important thing to understand is that the new covenant is for you. Understand that what it says, and Philippians 4:7 is the truth when it states, "and the peace of God, which surpasses all understanding, will guard your hearts and your minds through Christ Jesus." Remember what the peace of God is guarding your heart and mind against. It is the wrong teaching and doctrines of man.

With the acceptance of the new covenant, you will not listen to the misleading of men, and you will have a meaningful relationship with your Father, without the burdens of any law from the old covenant. But just as important as having a wonderful relationship, you will maintain a wonderful relationship with your Father that will not suffer because of some man-made doctrine of a works-righteous church.

3

The Two Commandments

With the new covenant of peace that was brought to us through the finished work of Jesus our Lord and Savior, a simpler understanding of all that is required of God's children was also revealed. Jesus took the original 613 laws of Moses and fulfilled them. And with that fulfillment, He gave us only two to follow. Matthew 22:36–40 says, "Teacher, which is the great commandment in the law?" And Jesus said to him, "You shall love the Lord your God with all your heart, with all your soul, and with all your mind." This is the first and great commandment. And the second is like it: "You shall love your neighbor as yourself. On these two commandments hang all the Law and the Prophets."

Mark 12:29–31 presents the same story but a little different because it tells us to love God with all of our strength also. So according to the teachings of Jesus, the most important thing we need to learn, in order to follow Him and have the same kind of wonderful Father-son relationship that Jesus had, is to love the way that Jesus loved. If we, as God's children, cannot understand love, then how can we understand the nature of God?

1 John 4:16 says, "And we have known and believed the love that God has for us. God is love, and he who abides in love abides in God, and God in him." According to this verse, we are to understand that love is the key to not only the character of God, but also it reveals His motivation and purpose for us.

In this chapter we will see that if you can learn to love the way that Jesus loved, which is the way that God intended us to love, you can walk in the same footsteps as our Lord and teacher Jesus Christ. You can have the same relationship with the Father that He has.

Now the first thing we need to do when looking at the prospect of learning how to love is to throw away most of what the world has told us that love is. The world's love is disposable; God's love is forever. The world's love is selfish; God's love is all-giving. Since there's only one true example of how to love, we will go to Him, our source. Let's take a look in scripture of how Jesus shows us how to love.

One of the first things we need to get out of the way is who we, as God's children, are required to love. This was the same question put to Jesus when He was asked who our neighbor is. Sadly, that is the first question that comes into the mind of a child of God today. *Who do I have to love? Who is our neighbor?*

Jesus made this very clear in Luke 10:25, which states, "And behold, a certain lawyer stood up and tested Him, saying, 'Teacher, what shall I do to inherit eternal life?'" In verse 26, Jesus asks him, "What is written in the law? What is your reading of it?" The lawyer answered correctly when he said in verse 27 to love your God and your neighbor. At this point in their conversation, Jesus said in verse 28, "You have answered rightly; do this and you will live."

But the man wanted to justify himself. In verse 29, he asks Jesus, "And who is my neighbor?" Verses 30–35 say, Then Jesus answered and said: "A certain man went down from Jerusalem to Jericho, and fell among thieves, who stripped him of his clothing, wounded him, and departed, leaving him half dead. Now by chance a certain priest came down that road. And when he saw him, he passed by on the other side. Likewise a Levite, when he arrived at the place, came and looked, and passed by on the other side. But a certain Samaritan, as he journeyed, came where he was. And when he saw him, he had compassion. So he went to him and bandaged his wounds, pouring on oil and wine: and he set him on his own animal, brought him to an inn, and took care of him. On the next day, when he departed, he took out two denarii, gave them to the innkeeper, and said to him, 'Take care of him; and whatever more you spend, when I come again, I will repay you.'"

And then Jesus asked the lawyer a very important question in verse 36: "So which of these three do you think was neighbor to him who fell among the thieves?" Verse 37 provides the answer. "And he said, 'He who showed mercy on him.' Then Jesus said to him, 'Go and do likewise.'"

It says in verse 29 that the lawyer wanted to justify himself. It is very important that we understand it is man's nature to take anything and try to justify it for his own benefit. If it is possible to justify why a person should or should not do something, they will, and this includes God's children. As I said before, we have to do away with the worldly understanding and totally embrace the teachings of Jesus.

So with these verses we understand who to love, according to Jesus. For a better understanding of who our neighbor is and who we are to love, we need to break down these versus. Jesus Himself has given us an example of who our neighbor is. And almost as important as who our neighbor is, we should examine the people who did nothing.

The first person in the story that passed by the half-dead man was a priest, a religious man of the time. We can agree that a priest was the righteous leader of the time. He was by his own definition a representative of the Heavenly Father, here on earth. He was, in fact, the earthly example of what man was to do in his relationship with God.

Recall that I said "by his own definition," because of everyone that Jesus taught about, His warnings about the religious leaders of that time were very clear. Jesus is definitely using the religious leader in this story as an example of what *not* to do. Too frequently in Jesus' time, as well as in the present, man looks to someone that we have placed upon a pedestal for our answers, and we believe that our religious leaders have those answers. Too many times we look to our church and its leaders and try to mimic them, because of their standing in the church. So everyone who listens to this story that Jesus is telling considers those people whom we already love, our teachers and friends, to be their neighbor.

We always call our friends and family "neighbors." When Jesus used the priest as an example, He knew that we would consider him our neighbor. Jesus talks in more detail about this subject in Mark 12:38–40, Luke 11:37–44, and also Luke 20:44–47. All of these verses speak of how the religious leaders do everything that they do for show. When they pray, it is for the people to see how religious they are. Jesus spoke many times about the hypocrisy of the religious leaders of His time, how they had no relationship with the Father. It talks about how on the outside they were clean, but on the inside they were "full of greed and wickedness." They are your neighbors; you're told to always love them. But never get the idea that you should be like them or that you should strive to be like any other neighbor who is walking in sin.

Next, scripture tells us that the Levites did the same thing as the priests. A Levite saw the man in the street, he knew that he needed help, but "he had not the love of God in him" either, so he crossed to the other side of the street, and went on his way. We know what kind of a man the Levite was. But let's take a look at what kind of a man he should have been. The Levites, as a people, were set aside for one purpose: to serve God and God's children. They came from the longest line of priests, from Levi, the third son of Jacob and Leah (Genesis 29:34).

Moses and Aaron were Levites of the family of Kohath, Levi's son. When land was divided among the Israelites, the Levites were assigned 48 towns in various tribal territories rather than a specific part of land (Joshua 21:1–8 and Numbers 35:2–7). The priestly class was to minister to the spiritual needs of the other tribes. So we can understand that a Levite was born and lived for one purpose, to serve God and help God's children.

Once again in the story, however, Jesus is pointing out that the person that we should be looking to for our teachings on how to love according to God and our neighbor, is not the religious leaders of our time. Jesus wants us to look at His teachings and that of His disciples. We are told that if anyone teaches anything different than the Gospel (Good News) of Jesus, it is wrong, and not what your Heavenly Father intended for you to be taught. You cannot add to or take away from His Word (Revelations 22:18–19).

The very worst part about the wrong teachings of religion today is it cannot set you free. It will not tell you who you are. It cannot give you the righteousness of God. It will, however, hinder you when you try to walk in the power that Jesus walked in. It will, in fact, make you doubt that you are even in the family of your Father. It will make you question where this peace is that everyone is talking about. It will make you run as fast as you can away from your Father and the wonderful relationship that waits for you with Him.

Now that we know how we should not act when showing love to our neighbor. Let's take a look at the man who stopped and helped the man left for dead. The Word says he was a Samaritan, and according to John 4:6–9, the hurt man would not have had anything to do with the Samaritan in any other place or time. We know this because of what the woman at the well said to Jesus in versus 6–9, "Now Jacob's well was there. Jesus therefore, being wearied from His journey, sat thus by the well. It was about the sixth hour. A woman of Samaria came to draw water. Jesus said to her, 'Give me a drink.' For His disciples had gone away into the city to buy food. Then the woman of Samaria said to Him, 'How is it that You, being a Jew, ask a drink from me, a Samaritan woman?' For Jews have no dealings with Samaritans."

The Samaritans were the inhabitants of the district of Samaria between Judah and Galilee. They were considered inferior by the Jews because of their mixed blood ancestry, going back to their intermarriage with foreign colonists, placed there by the Assyrians. See 2 Kings 17:3–24. The Jews had bad feelings toward the Samaritans. And we can understand that the negative feelings were mutual on the side of the Samaritans as well. And yet, the man who was clearly his enemy stopped and helped this dying Jew.

So in the case of who we are to love, we should think of the person or persons who rub us the wrong way. We should consider that the person or group of people that are unacceptable, hated, or despised are the person or people we are commanded to love. We are to look at the people of the world, not by what we consider to be right or wrong. Not to judge their actions, or their beliefs, not even what they say or do. We are to love that person or people, who, in our estimation, are unlovable.

Luke 6 tells us who to love, and verse 29 says, "To him who strikes you on the one cheek, offer the other also." Verse 30 takes it a step further and tells us who to give to, and what we should want in return. "Give to everyone who asks of you. And from him who takes away your goods do not ask them back."

And in the next verse (31), we are told how to measure the love that we have for our neighbor so that we know when to stop loving our neighbor. "And just as you want men to do to you, you also do to them likewise."

At this point in the story, most people start trying to justify the love that they don't have for their neighbor. They start by saying, "I have a lot of love. I love my family, my friends, all the people at the church, I even love most of the people at my work." But in verses 32, 33, and 34, we are told, "But if you love those who love you, what credit is that to you? For even sinners love those who love them. And if you do good to those who do good to you, what credit is that to you? For even sinners do the same. And if you lend to those from whom you hope to receive back, what credit is that to you? For even sinners lend to sinners to receive as much back."

Quite often, people, if they claim that they love everyone, they really mean they love everyone *from a distance*. Most people love by never having to deal with the people outside their own world, who are unlovable by religious standards. But in the previous verses, we are shown details on how we are to love these undesirable people of the world—with the same kind of love that we love those around us.

Luke 6:35 says, "But love your enemies, do good, and lend, hoping for nothing in return; and your reward will be great, and you will be sons of the Most High. For He is kind to the unthankful and evil." In this verse, Jesus is telling us many things about who to love, how to love, and why we should love.

Let us go first to the *why* we should love. It is very simple. If we ever hope to become true sons and daughters of God, we must first, without fail, learn to love. If we ever hope to walk in the power of God, we have no other way but to love. If we ever hope to use all the good gifts that God wants to give us, we must love. Love is as important to our own well-being as it is to the people we are to show that love to. If you truly want to understand and accept love, you must learn to give love.

We have been proving to ourselves through scripture who we are to love. We are to love all of God's children. And it tells us without a doubt that everyone on the earth is loved by God, even the "unthankful and evil."

First John 4:20, "If someone says, 'I love God,' and hates his brother, he is a liar; for he who does not love his brother whom he has seen, how can he love God whom he has not seen?" We must understand from this verse that the person that we are to love is *every person on God's earth*. The *why* we are to love is because without love we can never hope to really know God the Father or His nature. Because God is love, therefore, His nature must also be love.

4

That's Against My Nature

Jesus would not tell us to do something so hard, so against our "old man" nature without telling us how to do it. So in this chapter, we are going to learn the key to having not a worldly love, as we have been taught, but to have a godly love. The majority of the problem with the worldly love is it lacks the two main components that love must have in order to be from God and not from the world. These two essential components are forgiveness and compassion.

First, let us take a look at forgiveness. In Luke 6:36–42, it tells us how important that forgiveness is, both to our well-being and to the well-being of the world around us. Versus 36–37 say, "Therefore being merciful, just as your Father also is merciful. Judge not, and you shall not be judged. Condemn not, and you shall not be condemned. Forgive, and you will be forgiven."

Jesus tells us a story along the same lines of forgiveness in Matthew 18:23–35. The story tells of a king who wanted to settle an account with the servant who owed a great debt and that he was unable to pay. It was not like it is today, when you owe a debt to someone. There is really nothing that they can do to you, aside from asking you to pay. After all, the law protects you and your family from being put out on the street, much less being beaten or put in prison. But it was not that way in Jesus' time.

In the biblical days, a person could be sold to pay the debt, and not only he, but his wife and children could also be sold so that the debt could be paid. And everything that that man had or would ever have could be taken for the debt. And even though the king was well within his rights to do all of these things, it says in verse 27, "Then the master of that servant was moved with compassion, released him, and forgave him the debt."

Now upon hearing this story of the person who was forgiven such a great debt when he had so much to lose, you would think that this man would be happy and at peace. You would think after hearing this story about this man, that he would go out on the street, and with love in his heart, he would tell everyone how his life was changed because of the compassionate king and the forgiveness of his great debt. But in this story, Jesus tells about the reaction that the man had to the kindness shown him was just the opposite of what you would think that he would do. This man who stood to lose everything, this man the story says, went and found a fellow man who owed him a very small debt, and he grabbed him by the throat and said, "Pay me what you owe!" but the man could not pay the small debt. So the man who was forgiven his great debt had the man who owed him a small debt thrown "into prison till he should pay the debt."

Everyone knew what had happened, and someone told the king about what the man that he had forgiven had done to the man who owed him a small amount of money. So the king called the man before him that he had forgiven such a great debt. He showed him that his wrong against his fellow man was so great, that he, like the king, should have shown compassion on the one who owed him so little.

In verses 34 and 35, the end of this story is given. "And the master was angry, and delivered him to the torturers until he should pay all that was due to him. So My heavenly Father also will do to you if each of you, from his heart, does not forgive his brother his trespasses."

Forgiveness is not something that can be forced. Forgiveness comes through the realization of all that we have been forgiven of. In Matthew 10:8, Jesus is sending His disciples out into the world, as He has sent us out into the world. And He tells them what they need to do. He says, preach the kingdom of heaven is at hand, and "heal the sick, cleanse the lepers, raise the dead, cast out demons."

In verse 8, He says something that we must write on our heart as the truth. He says, "Freely you have received, freely give."

Now this is where we take a good hard look at all the Father has done to secure our future with Him here and in heaven. This is where we examine all that Jesus did that we might have a wonderful loving relationship with the Father through His finished work. This is where we stop and ask ourselves, what did salvation, good health, an abundant life, and a peaceful loving relationship with the Father cost me? And if you are truthful with yourself, you will realize at that moment, everything was a free gift, a gift given out of love from a Father to His beloved children. You will realize that it was free for you, but it was not free for everyone. It cost the Father His only begotten Son. It cost the Son to receive an undeserved punishment that would ultimately lead to His death. Yes, all that you have was a free gift for you and me. But it was by no means free to our Father, or for our Lord Jesus.

And upon further examination, you will find that there was no other reason, other than love, that they would have paid such a cost. And with this realization, you will understand that it is not that you have to love all of God's children. It is that with this realization you can't wait to love all of God's children. So like the man who was forgiven his debt, a great debt, we must forgive each and every debt that we have against our brother. "Freely we have received, freely give."

When you have trouble with this concept, the only thing you have to do is remember a time when you stood as the world stands—an orphan, lost, cold, and hungry, tired with no hope or faith in anything, because of who you were and how you lived. All that you need to do is remember back to a time when you were not a son or daughter of the Father. Think back when you did not have a relationship with the Creator of all things. Realize once again that all that you have, and all that you are, is because of the love that God your Father and Jesus your friend and brother showed to you.

The second thing that is so important in understanding how to bring out the love that God intended for His children to have is compassion. You will find that if you study and follow the teachings of Jesus Christ, He walked in love because of forgiveness and compassion.

An easy definition for compassion is putting yourself in the place of the person or people for a long enough time to feel what they feel, to know what they know, and to see what they see. To become them long enough that you begin to understand their pain, their anguish, and their longing to fill the emptiness in their lives.

In order to understand compassion, you have to put yourself in the place of those you do not love. And if you do this correctly, there will be forgiveness, and with forgiveness, there will be compassion, and with compassion, there will always be love.

Now in order to understand love, the way that we are told to love, you must first do away with our misconception of what the world perceives to be love. In order to do this, we need to go to 1 Corinthians 13. It tells how important love is, but also depending on the translation, how to judge if you really have compassion for God's children.

Yes, it talks of love, but mostly, it tells what love is not. Sometimes the best way to learn what to do is to observe and learn what not to do. Verses 1–3 tell us that all the works that we do for God, if done without love, mean nothing. "Though I speak with the tongues of men and of angels, but have not love, I have become sounding brass or a clanging cymbal. And though I have the gift of prophecy, and understand all mysteries and all knowledge, and though I have all faith, so that I could remove mountains, but have not love, I am nothing. And though I bestow all my goods to feed the poor, and though I give my body be burned, but have not love, it profits me nothing."

As we look at the first three verses in this chapter, we find that it says all the gifts of God, and any work that you do for God, are of no value without the kind of love that Jesus teaches us to have. Sure, you can speak in tongues; sure, you can work all the powers that Jesus told us that we would have when He left to be with the Father. You can know the Bible from the very first page of Genesis to the very last chapter in Revelations, you can give all that you have, or all that you ever will have. You can even die for your belief in God and Jesus. But if you don't have the kind of love that Jesus teaches us that we must have, then you're no more than just so much noise, and it will do you no good in the long run.

Verses 4–8 talk about love that is so unlike the example of the world's love that most people discount it or simply believe it does not apply to them. It speaks mostly of what love is not. The world's view is about what love is. The world's view of love consists of adding something to what they already have. The world teaches that if you add something to yourself, you will find love. But the teachings of Jesus explained in detail that if you remove yourself from the equation, then there's room for love.

The first line in verse 4 is not what the world wants to hear. "Love suffers long." The world does not like anything that might not give the appearance of pleasure. So it tells them right off that if you are to love, you must be willing to suffer long for that love, not just to be a little inconvenienced for a short time.

However, true love, taught to us by Jesus, knows no boundaries of time; that when you have the kind of love that we were always intended to have, it is strong and enduring, even through the hard times.

We fail when it comes to love because we have believed the definition of the world where love is concerned. Let's take marriage, for instance. When we get married, we take a vow to love that person no matter what. Just like all the promises of the world, there is a "but" in our given word. I promise to love you, *but*, when we have no money and times get hard, I will just leave. I promise to love you when you're sick, *but* if it becomes too much of a hardship, I quit. With God's love, there is no room for the word "but." And that is why the world rejects it.

We are children of God. We must learn never to say "but" when we are expressing His love. Always remember that the Father and His Son have suffered long for the love of His children. Also know that all the joy and fulfillment that you have always wanted to experience with the world's love can now be yours when you learn how to love the way that Jesus teaches us to love. You will understand that almost everything that has gone wrong in your life up to this point was because you were trying to apply the love that the world teaches to all the situations of your life. When you learn how to love as God intended you to love, you will truly find peace.

Verses 4–8 tell us how to judge if we really do have the love of God in us or not. It tells us what to look for in our walk. It tells us how to love the way Jesus loves us. Verse 4 states, "love does not envy." To be envious is to want to be like that other person, to want to have what they have. But envy is not love. And because it is not love, it will not last; it will not endure.

There was a man who saw a coat that another man was wearing. And he said to himself, "If I had that man's coat, I would look as good as he looks. If I had that man's coat, I would have numerous friends, just as that man has. If I only had that man's coat I would have the money and power which that man has." So the man plotted and eventually beat the man and took the coat. But when he put the coat on, there was no change in his life. As a matter of fact, nothing changed except now he was wearing a stolen coat. And as he observed the man who he had beaten to steal his coat, he noticed that nothing in that man's life changed either, because, after all, it's just a coat.

It sounds silly, doesn't it? That a man would look at what another man has, and because of something that he wears, drives, or lives in, he feels that this man is a better man than himself. I found in my life that the grass does look greener on the other side of the fence. But that appearance is deceiving because of what we perceive the grass to be. The truth is it is not greener.

If you want to change your life and the way you live that life, if you are trying to become that person you've always wanted to be, the only way is to learn to love. It all comes down to "love suffers long and is kind; love does not parade itself, is not puffed up; does not behave rudely, does not seek its own, is not provoked, thinks no evil; love does not rejoice in iniquity, but rejoices in the truth; bears all things, believes all things, hopes all things, endures all things" (verses 4–7). And the very most important thing to remember: "Love never fails" (verse 8). This is nothing less than a list of how to judge oneself by what Jesus teaches us, and not what the world teaches us.

We have been told many places in scripture to love our Father and to love our neighbor. We learned that everyone in the world is our neighbor. We learn how to love, because we learned what love is not. We learn to filter our definition of love through the love of the Father and the teachings of Jesus. We learn not to judge the world, but to have compassion for the world. And with having true compassion, you can't help but have that love that we were always intended to have.

Please understand that as with all the gifts that God gives us, you will receive greater benefits for yourself than anything you could possibly give to the world. That in return for learning how to love, you will be filled with the joy, peace, and contentment that nothing but love can give you. And you will achieve the most important thing in your walk with the Father.

James 1:12 says, "Blessed is the man who endures temptation; for when he has been approved, he will receive the crown of life which the Lord has promised to those who love Him." Always remember that everything in your walk with the Father hinges on love, not knowledge, not works—just love.

5

The Inheritance
of the King's Son

Many people today are under the misconception that when Jesus left this earth to go to be the Father, that all the power and authority that He and His disciples used here on earth went with Him when He left. In other words, they believe that Jesus gave us a job to do, but did not give us any power or authority to do that job.

Nothing could be further from the truth. When you think about this statement, it doesn't even make sense. Let's say, for instance, that you owned a large successful company and you realize that you need to delegate some of the burden of responsibility to another person. You then pick the person that you're going to give this responsibility to. You call that person into your office, and you explain what the job will entail. This person accepts the responsibility of the job. But then, at the last minute, you tell them, "By the way, you have no power or authority over any part of my company." Now, the first thing that would go through the mind of any reasonable or logical person is *I cannot do the job if you do not give me the power and authority to do the job.* That is why it is so ludicrous to listen to the wrong teachings of any religious doctrine that states this. We were not left to do this job without any power or authority from God.

As I have said, we (God's children) were intended to have dominion (have power) over the earth. Adam gave away this power and authority for a short time. But it was brought back by Jesus through His finished work.

We see a demonstration of the power that God intended to give us through Jesus in Luke 9, where Jesus is explaining to His 12 disciples how to go out into the world and do the job that He has given them. It says in verse 1, after He had called them altogether. He "gave them power and authority over all demons, and to cure diseases." Verse 2 states, "He sent them to preach the kingdom of God and to heal the sick."

It is very important that we understand that God has never given a job to anyone where He did not give them every single tool and the knowledge that would be needed to complete the job. Once again, this teaching of being left without help is contrary to God's nature.

No one that looks at the Father through the eyes of love and forgiveness could possibly think that the Father would give you something to do, then just watch you fail. Our Father has always wanted His children to succeed. And all of scripture states that He has gone out of His way to see that this would happen.

The problem with this erroneous teaching is, if you come to the realization that you have everything you need to do the work and live the life that Jesus commanded you to live, that with this understanding of who you are and what you have been given, you have no excuse why you're not doing what you were told to do. You cannot blame God the Father for the way your life is, because you are in charge of your life. You cannot blame the devil for the circumstances you are in because he is already defeated and has no power other than the power that you relinquish to him. You cannot say, "I didn't know what to do," because God's Word (the Bible) is one of the most sold books in the world, and is available to anyone that desires to know the truth. That only leaves *you* to take responsibility for not living the life, and for not doing the job that you were left here on earth to accomplish.

The fact that God has always given us everything that was needed to complete the work that He left to be done for His children did not change with the finished work that was given to Jesus to do. Jesus was given everything that He needed to complete His work that was given to Him by God the Father. And in that same line of thinking, the job or work that was given to us to do by our Lord Jesus is no different. "And the Holy Spirit descended in bodily form like a dove upon Him, and a voice came from heaven which said, 'You are My beloved Son; in You I am well please'" (Luke 3:22). This verse states plainly that God sent the Holy Spirit to help with the work that Jesus was about to begin for God and man. We too were given a Spirit to help us in this world, to accomplish the work given to us by Jesus.

As a matter of fact, we were given the same Spirit that was given to Jesus by God. Not a different spirit of lesser ability. John 16:7 says, "Nevertheless I tell you the truth. It is to your advantage that I go away; for if I do not go away, the Helper will not come to you; but if I depart, I will send Him to you." This Spirit, or Helper, as He is called here, is the same Spirit that was in Jesus as a Helper for Him to finish the work that the Father had given Him to do. We can understand that because Jesus was almost done with His work that the Father gave Him to do here on earth, and that He (Jesus) would soon be able to pass to us this Helper so that man (you and I) might accomplish the work of the Father given to us by Jesus.

There is only one Spirit as it says in 1 Corinthians 12:4, "There are diversities of gifts, but the same Spirit." Verse 11 states, "But one and the same Spirit works all these things, distributing to each one individually as He wills." Verse 13 says, "For by one Spirit we were all baptized into one body—whether Jews or Greeks, whether slaves or free—and have all been made to drink into one Spirit." It is plain to see that there is only one Spirit, and that He was sent from God.

Nowhere in scripture does it say that He will leave us or that He will stop helping us to do the work of the Father—ever. On the contrary, it says in Romans 8:2-11, that because of the Spirit we have an abundance of wonderful gifts, fit for the son of the King.

We have been given freedom from the law, because the righteous requirements are fulfilled. Now we walk in the Spirit not in the flesh because of the Spirit. We please God the Father because it is His Spirit and His righteousness that are in us. You have abundant life because the spirit is life, and because of

God's righteousness that lives in you. The Father's Spirit is in you, the same Spirit who raised Christ from the dead and He will give life to your mortal body. It is by this Spirit, not your strength or will, that you are able to put to death the deeds of the body and then you will live the life of peace and joy that you were always destined to live.

The Spirit of God was put inside you, to lead you, to show you the right way to do the job that was given to you. The Spirit is always there to edify you, to build you up. The Spirit of God was given to us by God the Father, and He will always, without fail, be there to help you do the work. He will show you what you need to do the job, and then He will roll up His sleeves and help you do the work. He is never negative, condemning, or judgmental. So if you think at any time that the Spirit of God is doing any of these things, you are mistaken. That negative nature is not the Spirit of God that you are listening to. Romans 8:14 states, "For as many as are led by the Spirit of God, these are sons of God."

So are we to understand from these verses that all believers have the same Spirit, the same power, as Jesus? Yes! Absolutely and without a doubt, scripture tells us that we are sons of God because we have the Father's Spirit in us.

We must understand that the Spirit that dwells inside of every believer is the Spirit of our Father. And that the Spirit of our Father is a Spirit of freedom from bondage. It is a Spirit free from fear. It is a spirit of adoption, and with this knowledge and understanding provided by this gentle Spirit of our Father that resides in you, you will come to understand that God the Father calls us not just to His royal presence, but to run to Him as His loved child. And because of this status of an adopted son and daughter, now He wants the kind of relationship of a Father with His child. He wants you to come to Him out of love, to climb up into His lap, hug His neck, and let Him love on you and for you to call Him "Abba Father," which simply means "Daddy."

The doctrine of today tells us that our Father is not reachable. This is a wrong teaching. You need to understand that God your Father is exactly that: He is your Father, your Daddy. You can never hope to have the kind of relationship with your Father that He has always intended for you to have with Him if you can't grasp this concept.

When the apostle Paul wrote to the Corinthians, he was trying to explain who they were now that they were a child of God. He explains in chapter 2 that through the Spirit of God that lives in each and every one of us, that we can know the nature of God our Father.

1 Corinthians 2:9–16 says, "Eye has not seen, nor ear heard, nor have entered into the heart of man the things which God has prepared for those who love Him.'But God has revealed them to us through His Spirit. For the Spirit searches all things, yes, and the deep things of God. For what man knows the things of a man except the spirit of the man which is in him? Even so no one knows the things of God except the Spirit of God. Now we have received, not the spirit of the world, but the Spirit who is from God, that we might know the things that have been freely given to us by God. These things we also speak, not in words which man's wisdom teaches but which the Holy Spirit teaches, comparing spiritual things with spiritual. But the natural man does not receive the things of the Spirit of God, for they are foolishness to him; nor can he know them, because they are spiritually discerned. But he who is spiritual judges all things, yet he himself is rightly judged by no one. For who has known the mind of the Lord that he may instruct Him?' But we have the mind of Christ."

There are several very important points that we must assimilate into who we are if we are to become who God intended us to be. In these verses it is critical that you realize the importance of the word "but." Because if you just read these verses without understanding what the word "but" means, then the whole meaning will be lost. The word "but" all through the Bible means "everything before this word is null and void."

I will elaborate further in another chapter, but for the purpose of understanding these verses, it is essential that you understand the meaning of the word "but." For instance, in the beginning of these verses, it states that no eye or ear can understand things which God has prepared for His children that love Him. This verse is from Isaiah, and if you stop here, you would never understand that this verse has been fulfilled by the finished work of Jesus Christ.

Now we need to look at the next verse, which starts with the word "but." In this verse, it states that because of the Spirit of God that dwells in us, all the things that God has for His children have now been revealed. He goes on to say that it is not just the simple, easy things that have been revealed; it is the deep things that man has never known before that have now been shown to man. And it's all because of the Spirit of God that resides in us. It says, with all of this knowledge that is provided to us by God's Spirit, we now know all the things that have been provided freely by God.

We need to examine one single word in this line and understand it completely. The word "freely." Everything that the Spirit has informed you that you possess has been provided by your Father for His children as a free gift. This simply means you cannot pay for what you have, so stop trying, and just use the gifts from your Father. It also says in these verses that a lot of worldly people will not understand that now, because of our status as adopted children, we are different than not only everyone else in the world, but different than any creature has been since Adam. It is the world, or the natural man, that will not understand. They will look at this and perceive it as foolishness because they do not recognize God's Spirit that dwells in us.

It goes on to say that you are right in your thinking, and that no man has the right to judge you now, because you have the mind of Christ. If you feel pretty special now, you should; after all, we have determined that you not only have the Spirit of God in you, but that you also have the mind of Christ in you.

The Spirit that resides in us makes "intercession for us" when we are weak and don't know how to go to the Father or what to say when we get there. The Spirit of God is an eternal guide. It was given to us by our Father Himself to make everything that we do easier, both in our relationship with our Father and our relationship with our fellow man. The problem is, we still have a free choice of whom we will listen to. And because of that free choice, we don't always go in the direction that the Spirit would lead us. But by understanding the loving nature of your Father and the nature of His Spirit, you will find that the decisions that you make, when filtered through this viewpoint of who the Father is, will always be right. Because, after all, you are making the decisions with the help of your Father's indwelling Spirit in you.

The Spirit of God does all of this so that we might be protected from the condemnation of the world and that we may accept the fact that because of the many wonderful gifts provided by our Father through the finished work of our Lord Jesus, that "we are children of God," "and if children, then heirs—heirs of God and joint heirs with Christ" (Romans 8:16–17). If you are a believer, then you are a son or daughter of the God that created everything. The only thing left for you to do with this information is to realize who you are and start acting like God's adopted child.

6

Another Gift from the King

Along with the Spirit, another gift that was given to us by our Father as a powerful tool to accomplish the work that Jesus commanded us to do is His Word. The power of God's Word is one of the most amazing gifts that was given to us by our Father. And just as it is with the gift of His Spirit, the Word is a tool used by our Lord Jesus in the completion of His work. It says in scripture that God Himself used His Word to create everything that was created. Jesus used His Word to defeat Satan after fasting in the desert. With His Word, His children have been doing the work of the Father, even before Jesus went to sit at God's right hand. Hebrews 4:12 says, "For the word of God is living and powerful, and sharper than any two-edged sword."

The religious leadership of today would have you believe that the power to work in the same realm as the first-century church was lost somewhere along the way. And in a way it was. It does not work as it was intended to work, just like a power tool would not work if never plugged into an electrical outlet because the person using the power tool was convinced, by someone they trusted and believed, that there was no power in the outlet. Therefore, the power tool was rendered useless to the person because the information provided to them by someone they trusted was invalid. So even though the only restriction that they had on the use of the power tool was misinformation, it was sufficient to keep them from utilizing the powerful tool that they possessed.

This is very similar to what is happening to God's children today. They have, through the misinformation of people that they trusted, come to believe and understand that there is no power for God's children here on earth. Nothing ever taught to man has been so far from the truth. The power is—and has always been—available for God's children. They simply refuse to believe, that the power exists, and therefore, cannot tap into it. So the very first thing that we must do is to expel all of the erroneous ideas that the world has taught about the power of God in you.

You must understand that the failure to utilize the power that God provided for His children rests on their choices and beliefs. It is man's choice not to use all of the gifts provided to us by our Father. We must understand that it is not God who keeps us from utilizing these wonderful gifts. It is the fact that we refuse to believe that there is power in the outlet. And thus, we never plug in the tool that was provided by the Father.

We must understand that it is not God our Father who withholds anything from us. It is what we have come to believe that inhibits us. You must understand that for whatever reason this corrupt doctrine was introduced, it has crippled the work and the abundant life that was given to every disciple of Jesus Christ.

I'm sorry to say that many of the reasons for the corruption in the Gospel are because of greed and power, much like the wealth and power that were attained by the religious leaders of Jesus' day. Many of our religious leaders of today have the same affliction.

Just as the Jewish religious leaders refused to see what was written about the coming of the Messiah, our religious leaders, because of wealth and power, refuse to believe that every man can have all of the wonderful gifts that have been talked about in the Holy Book, as a free gift with no charge or works on their part. Because if we, as the masses, were to realize just how easy it is to become a part of the most wonderful family ever conceived since the beginning of time, we might not feel the need to give money to support our religious leaders' mansions, their Cadillac Escalades, their fine clothes or any other extravagance that they feel so worthy of, because they have misled all of God's children for their benefit.

If you truly understand who you are in God's family, you would have no need to teach such a lie as guilt, fear, and condemnation because these are the tools that the religious community has always used to attain their much-sought-after power and wealth. If the people were ever to realize, that they are equal with every single person on earth, and that this includes the highest self-exalted clergy, religion would lose its grip because the ignorance of their lies would be exposed. A lie can only exist in the darkness of ignorance.

Always remember, you are a child of God, a servant of man. We were left here to do a job, the job that was summed up by Jesus when He told us to love and do for all others who have a need the same way that you would want them to do for you if you have a need.

There is one other reason why the religious leaders have misled God's children for thousands of years. They believe that the gifts from God were not enough to solve the problem of sin. So they have twisted God's Word to a point where it is unrecognizable. You could say in their defense they had the right motive. But because of their lack of faith in God's ability to fix the problem of sin, once again, they've just made it worse.

History teaches us that fear of punishment does not work as a deterrent to sin. If it did, there would be no need for prisons because fear would alleviate crime. The fear of God has never drawn man to God. In fact, the fear of judgment and punishment have always made man run from God. So any time you hear a teaching or doctrine along these lines, ask yourself, is this the Gospel?

Ephesians 4:13–15 states, "till we all come to the unity of the faith and of the knowledge of the Son of God, to a perfect man, to the measure of the stature of the fullness of Christ; that we should no longer be children, tossed to and fro and carried about with every wind of doctrine, by the trickery of men, in the cunning craftiness of deceitful plotting, but, speaking the truth in love, may grow up in all things into Him who is the head—Christ."

God's plan was simple. His plan was to make every single person on the earth a prince or princess of the Highest King. When you are exalted to that station or stature, you have no reason to break the law because you answer to a higher standard than the law. You answer to the standard of love. Our Lord

Jesus refrained from sin not because He feared what God would do to Him, but because He knew who He was, because He knew who the Father was. Basically, there was no room for sin in His life because everything He did, He did because of love—not law.

By now, you're probably saying to yourself, I thought he was going to explain about the gift of God's Word. And I am. But if you do not filter God's Word through the loving nature of your Father, you will not only fail to use this wonderful gift, but you will also hurt yourself in the trying. You must understand that the adversary will twist the Word, as he tried to do with Jesus in the desert. His tactics have not changed from the beginning, when he tempted God's children in the Garden. So it is extremely important that you understand the meaning of God's Word. And this can only be done through a filter of love. So anything that you read in God's Word must be filtered through the knowledge of who God is. And ironically, we see who God is through the Word and the example that Jesus set forth for us while He was here on earth.

Why is the Word so powerful? Because it's living! "For the word of God is living and powerful" (Hebrews 4:12). Every word that God spoke went forth with power, and not only that, but it is still going forth and doing what God wanted it to do, with no lack of power or momentum. "So shall My word be that goes forth from My mouth; it shall not return to Me void, but it shall accomplish what I please, and it shall prosper in the thing for which I sent it" (Isaiah 55:11). We must always remember that God's Word never loses power or intent. That whatever God's purpose was when He spoke it, is still as valid today as it was at that moment. It cannot be changed or altered in any way. It will accomplish what God wants it to accomplish.

First Peter 1:23 says, "having been born again, not of corruptible seed but incorruptible, through the word of God which lives and abides forever." So we are to understand that it is through the Word that we are able to be born-again.

Here's where you say to yourself. "I always knew that there was power in God's Word when He spoke it. He is God! What does this have to do with me? I'm not God!" And I'm sorry to say, this is the popular view of the church today, that the power of the Word of God is only for God. That common man should never even try to use something that was only intended for the super-religious for the superanointed. This too is a misconception sent down from the church.

The third-century church exalted a handful of men and claimed that their status was given to them by God. This is a lie! But because of this lie, we continue to place men in a position neither warranted nor deserved. We have too long exalted people like the Pope, leaders of large organized religions, and even TV evangelists to a stature that can only be harmful to the spreading of the Gospel. This is *not* scriptural; this is *not* the Word of God.

The Word of God was given to every single child of God so that His work could be done through His Word. So not only are we allowed to use God's Word, we are expected to know *how* to use God's Word, and to utilize every single Word from the mouth of God. He generously gave us this gift, of His Word, that we might accomplish the job given to us by Jesus.

Jesus, in fact, tells us that the Word of God is more important to your survival and well-being than the food that you eat or the air that you breathe. "Man shall not live by bread alone, but by every word that proceeds from the mouth of God" (Matthew 4:4).

Using God's Word is not a new thing. As I said before, Jesus used the knowledge of God's Word to fight the adversary, Satan. When He said those words, He was quoting from Deuteronomy 8:3. The Word has always been powerful, and it has always been available to man, but never more so than since the finished work of Jesus Christ.

So how do we use this powerful tool? You could say it works automatically, but even with something that is automatic, you must do something to get it started. You have to at least take it out of the box, push a button to get it started, or pull a trigger.

It's the same way with using the Word of God effectively. First, you must learn what the Father really said. You must receive the knowledge through a heart of understanding the nature of your Father. What I mean by that statement is if you hear or read anything that does not line up with the love of your Father, it is not the meaning that was intended. Either you are reading it wrong, due to a lack of understanding your Father's nature, or you are being taught incorrectly by someone that you apparently trust. Everything that you do on your journey as a child of God should be to strive for a more intimate relationship with your Heavenly Father because this is the only way to learn how loving and forgiving He is.

Second Timothy 1:13 says, "Hold fast the pattern of sound words which you have heard from me, in faith and love which are in Christ Jesus." We should always filter all teachings and knowledge through the understanding of God's goodness and love. Because if you do anything different than this, you will gain a misunderstanding of not only who the Father is but also a misconception of who you are. And with this confusion, you will never be able to rest in the peace that can only be found in the Father's love.

Second Timothy 2:15 says, "Be diligent to present yourself approved to God, a worker who does not need to be ashamed, rightly dividing the word of truth." You will not accept judgment from anyone with the correct understanding of God's Word.

So how do you divide the Word of God so that it will be of use in your endeavor to go forth and do the Father's work? The easiest way to understand how to use this gift is to go back to the basics. To look at it in a natural way instead of a superspiritual way.

When we were children in school, there was a basic teaching that said, "You are what you eat." This simply stated the fact that what your body ingests has something to do with your physical makeup. Your body will process whatever food you put into it and eventually alter what you physically become.

The same is true with the Word of God. Jesus said, "Man shall not live by bread alone, but by every word that proceeds from the mouth of God" (Matthew 4:4). In order to live on the bread that you eat, you must first ingest the bread, and then the body will process it into the different parts as it is needed. This is the same with the Word of God. If you do not take it into your heart through your mind, you will not become everything that you were intended to be. If you never ingest the bread (i.e., the Word), then not everything that it was intended to do for you can be accomplished. "Let the word of Christ dwell in you richly in all wisdom" (Colossians 3:16). "And have tasted the good word of God and the powers of the age to come" (Hebrews 6:5).

Jesus tells us in order to have the Word abiding in you, you must first believe in Him. John 5:38 states, "But you do not have His word abiding in you, because whom He sent, Him you do not believe." So it is plain that the

Word must become a part of who you are, and then you will become part of the Word of God. In order to do this, you must first believe in Jesus and His finished work.

As I have said before, you will only accept what you believe to be true, not what you read or what you hear. It is because of the Word that we become a new person. As it says in 1 Peter 1:23, "having been born again, not of corruptible seed but incorruptible, through the word of God which lives and abides forever." The Word has power that lasts forever, but if you never get the Word of God inside of you, if you never let the Word of God do its work in you, then you're in line with most of the religious world. They stand with the Bible in their hand, looking toward the heavens with the look of a defeated child, wondering why God doesn't do something, never knowing the power that they hold is more than sufficient to handle any and all problems, but that this power just lies dormant for lack of knowledge and understanding.

We should never, as children of God our Father, assume that we are not in charge of this world that He has given us. We were given stewardship over this world. We were given a job to do. And we were given all the tools that we would need to do that job. We should never act defeated or helpless in the face of any wrong that this world has to bring against us. Isaiah 54:16–17 says, "'Behold I have created a blacksmith who blows the coals in the fire, who brings forth an instrument for his work; and I have created the spoiler to destroy. No weapon formed against you shall prosper, and every tongue which rises against you in judgment you shall condemn. This is the heritage of the servants of the Lord, and their righteousness is from Me,' says the Lord."

We are children of God, the God who created everything. There is nothing that was created that was not created by your Heavenly Father. When we were adopted into God's family, we were endowed with all the gifts, rights, and privileges befitting a son and daughter of the King. All that we, as His children, have to do is to take advantage of this position and to realize and accept the fact of who we are and start to become everything that our Father has always intended for us to be.

7

It's Not What You Know, It's What You Believe

I am always amazed at the amount of people that I meet who have been going to church for many years and who really do not know what they believe. Or worse than that, they don't know why they believe what they believe. It is fascinating to stand and listen to the conversations that people have about the Bible and its contents.

People often talk about scripture, really believing that their argument has some validity according to the contents of the Bible, when, in fact, it is just something that has been said so much by the churchgoing public that they have indoctrinated it into their teaching about the Bible.

I have often stood and listened to quotes, supposedly out of the Bible, only to realize although they were very wise quotes, they were from such men as Benjamin Franklin and even Albert Einstein. I cannot tell you how many times I have heard "spare the rod and spoil the child." This is not a quote from scripture. Someone has taken the concept that we need to bring up our children with fear as opposed to love. Actually, the scripture that prompted this particular mind-set was "He who spares his rod hates his son, But he who loves him disciplines him promptly." (Proverbs 13:24)

We have a misconception of the word "discipline." We misconstrue this word and believe it to mean punishment. The fact is that if you are a disciplined child, there is no need for punishment. Therefore, when it says in Proverbs 22:6, "Train up a child in the way he should go, And when he is old he will not depart from it." This simply means if you do your job of teaching discipline to your children, there will be no reason to punish them. This is only one small misinterpretation in the thousands of misinterpretations that we have taken into our heart as a wrong belief.

Most, if not all, of the problems with a wrong belief is misinformation about God the Father and what His Word really means. It is easy to misunderstand the meaning of this word if you misunderstand His loving nature. If at any time you forget that your Father is never mad at you, that He never judges you, and that He always wants only the best for you, then you will tend to read His Word through a cloud of judgment and condemnation. This will always change the way you receive His Word. And, in turn, you will write an untrue belief on your heart.

It was because of this misinterpretation of God's Word that the religious leaders at the time of Jesus' ministry so emphatically denied the truth that the Messiah had come. They had misread, and therefore, distorted the meaning of God's Word in such a way that anyone would have had a hard time recognizing the true nature of God. They had taught for thousands of years an untruth about the Messiah, what He would actually accomplish here on earth, and because of this misguided belief that was written in their hearts, they would not let go of their preconceived idea of how everything would be fulfilled.

So when Jesus came to earth and He was not what they had decided He should be, they rejected Him. Even with the proof in front of their eyes, they were blind to the fact that here in front of them was God's Son, sent to do exactly what they had been reading about for all of those years. And because of their refusal to rewrite the truth on their hearts, they would forfeit their salvation and their peace with their Father.

If any of this sounds vaguely familiar to you, it is because this is precisely what is happening because of religion today. Because of the blindness brought on by ignorance, power, and greed, God's children are being kept in the dark about who they really are in God's family, and what was, and still is, their birthright. Because of the misconception and misinterpretation of God's Word and all of the man-made doctrines created by religion, mankind has made the choice to stay bound, never knowing of the freedom, love, and power that await them.

So we can understand that nothing has any validity until we believe it in our heart as a truth. Everyone believes something. Everyone has at least a small amount of belief about any given thing.

Our very first part of the belief system is one that I feel that most people in the world have. It is a belief that God exists. Hebrews 11:6 says, "But without faith it is impossible to please Him, for he who comes to God must believe that He is, and that He is a rewarder of those who diligently seek Him."

We must understand, that every person that worships in any Christian church has the basic belief that God is real, but according to these versus, you need to seek Him out. The one thing that most churches don't tell you is the reason why you need to seek Him out. It's very simple. It's the same reason that His children have always looked for Him, to establish a loving relationship with Him. If you never look for your Father, you will never find your Father. ". . . seek, and you will find; knock, and it [the door] will be opened to you" (Matthew 7:7).

Let's say, for instance, you go to visit a friend. When you arrive at their home, you expect to see their car in the driveway, but as you come closer to the house, you see that the driveway is empty. At this point, you determine that they are not home. So you decide with this newfound knowledge to write a note and leave it on the door. You write the note, a little annoyed because you came all this way for nothing. You place the note on the door, you get in your car, and drive away. The truth of this situation was that your friend was inside the house all along. He had dropped his car off at the shop and was waiting inside the house for your arrival.

Your friend had, in fact, prepared your favorite meal. He had invited you over for one purpose, that you and all of your friends might celebrate your newfound wealth which was to be announced upon your arrival. They were anxiously waiting for your knock on their door. But because you have believed an untruth, brought on by misinformation, you never knocked on the door, and therefore, failed to receive all the good that was waiting for you on the other side of that door.

This is exactly what has happened to God's children. They have failed to knock on the door, believing that nothing more than salvation waits for them on the other side. If as His child you believe in your heart that He is not there or that he has nothing for you, you will never knock.

You might tell yourself, "I do not see a problem with my church. My beliefs are founded on scripture, and I have that loving relationship with my Father that you're so adamant about." And I would say to you that this is the most wonderful news I could hear about your life. But you are not the majority; on the contrary, you are a part of a small minority of Christians in the world today. I would also say that you need to be educating those poor misinformed people about the truth that you know or meet every day.

But as for the rest of us, we need to look at some of the criteria for being a child of God and having all of the peace and contentment that goes with that title. First of all, let us look at the way we, as God's children, act and react toward both the world and the rest of His children.

It appears that most Christians believe the first part of Hebrews 11:6, that there is a God. But many of His children fail to believe that He wants to give them a reward for simply finding Him and establishing a relationship with Him. Most religious people tend to say things like, "Sure, I believe, but..."

The very first lesson on belief is there is no "but" when it comes to belief. Once you have inserted a "but" after any statement of belief, it means everything I said, thought, or believed is now changed to doubt. And the word "doubt" in the Greek language means an effort to withdraw from or to oppose. So when we doubt, we separate or withdraw from God with opposition to what He wants.

Because of unbelief, you will have doubt, and that doubt will cause you to oppose God and what He truly wants for you.

Jesus tells us how important it is for us to believe without doubt. When He is teaching His disciples a lesson about belief and doubt in Matthew 21:19, "And seeing a fig tree by the road, He came to it and found nothing on it but leaves, and said to it, Let no fruit grow on you ever again.' Immediately the fig tree withered away." Verses 20–21 state, " And when the disciples saw it, they marveled, saying, 'How did the fig tree wither away so soon?' So Jesus answered and said to them, 'Assuredly, I say to you, if you have faith and do not doubt, you will not only do what was done to the fig tree, but also if you say to this mountain, "Be removed and cast into the sea," it will be done.'" Verse 22 concludes with "And whatever things you ask in prayer, believing, you will receive."

It is because of your belief that faith is able to work. What you believe goes into your heart, and eventually you become a culmination of your beliefs. A person will always levitate toward what he or she truly believes in their heart. Hebrews 3:12 says it this way: "Beware, brethren, lest there be in any of you an evil heart of unbelief in departing from the living God."

Doubt or unbelief separates us from God not because of what you do, but because of what you really believe in your heart. Hebrews 3:17–19 goes on to say that God's children could not enter into the rest that God had provided for them because of unbelief. Verse 19 states, "So we see that they could not enter in because of unbelief." This is the same problem that most of God's children have today as well. They cannot enter into the peace and rest given to them as a free gift by the finished work of our Lord Jesus. And the main reason for this is a misinterpretation of the Word of God and the misunderstanding of His nature.

When man first began to interpret the meaning of God's Word, he filtered it through what he believed to be God's nature. They believed that God's nature was to judge, strike down, and bring terror and fear to man, so that man would live a righteous life. What they did not understand is that God did what He had to do because of the law. They did not understand when interpreting His Word that His nature has always been that of love and forgiveness. But because the law had to be satisfied, He was forced into a position of judgment.

But now with the finished work of our Lord Jesus Christ, our Heavenly Father can, and does, show His true nature to the world. The problem is that man still wants to interpret God's Word as though all judgment of sin had not been fulfilled by Jesus. I am here to tell you that without a doubt, every sin which brought that judgment has been satisfied by Jesus.

Now we must look at God's nature through the eyes of love, and not the eyes of judgment. We must use this filter of love to determine and define what the true nature of God is, and therefore, have a truer understanding of God's Word and we will be led to the kind of belief that brings us to a loving relationship with our Father.

If you have any questions about what kind of a relationship you should have with your Father, simply study the way that Jesus reacted to His Father. You are to have that same relationship with our Father. He is the same God that Jesus turned to every day of His life. He talked to Him as His Father. He talked about Him as His Father. Part of what made the religious leaders of Jesus' time so angry was that He claimed to have a personal relationship with God as His Son—because He *did* have a personal relationship with God. And I will make you one promise, that when you achieve the same kind of relationship with your Heavenly Father as Jesus had, all the ultrareligious people will claim that you blasphemy just like the ultrareligious people of Jesus' day claimed He did.

In our language you have many choices of the right definition of any particular word. This was, and is, the same with the Greek, Hebrew, and Aramaic languages, where all of the translations for God's Word originated. So how do we know what the proper translation is? By knowing the nature of our Father and His intentions toward His children, you will understand the meaning behind His Word.

There are many misinterpretations in scripture because the people defining the Word of God did not know God's nature. One example of this misinterpretation is found in Matthew 11:29: "Take My yoke upon you and learn from Me, for I am gentle and lowly in heart, and you will find rest for your souls." Too often, the religious world has taken one word and changed the meaning of that word, which, in turn, changes the meaning of the entire thought. In this case, it is the word "yoke." For a long time, the church was taught that the yoke was a coupling for animals to work together. And yes, that is one of the definitions in the Greek language. But it is not the only definition for the word "yoke."

Another definition is a law or an obligation. When you read this verse, with the understanding that the yoke that Jesus is talking about is a different law or obligation other than the one that they are currently under, then you begin to see that with Jesus' teaching, you obtain the rest that He is talking about: "For My yoke [law or obligation] is easy and My burden is light" (Matthew 11:30). But with this teaching we would be calling Jesus a liar if we find that being one of His disciples was hard. Because, after all, Jesus said it was easy, but because Jesus cannot lie, there must be some other reason why it is so hard to enter into this rest.

The only other thing it could be is the fact that you did not take on His law or obligation. And if you didn't trade the law or obligation that you are living under now for His law and obligation, then you must still be living by some other law and obligation, not His. Chances are, you are trying to hold on to a law or doctrine imposed by religion. "Stand fast therefore in the liberty by which Christ has made us free, and do not be entangled again with a yoke [law or obligation] of bondage" (Galatians 5:1).

If any doctrine of any religion keeps you down with fear, judgment, or condemnation, even self-condemnation, it is not the teaching of our Lord and Savior Jesus Christ. It is the teaching of a misguided, uninformed doctrine. Remember, the only problem there has ever been with any of God's plans— was man.

Always remember to filter every word you read and hear through the never-ending love and forgiveness of our Father. Not through what some self-exalted, superspiritual, ultrareligious person believes to be true. Simply look to your Father and ask Him to show you the truth of what He wants for you and what His nature is. And then, all that is left for you to do is to believe that He will show you the truth. And according to His Word, His truth and wisdom will always be yours. And with that knowledge, provided by the Father, you will become wise. After all, wisdom is no more than knowledge that has been applied to your life because of belief.

James 1:5–7 says it this way: "If any of you lacks wisdom, let him ask of God, who gives to all liberally and without reproach, and it will be given him. But let him ask in faith, with no doubting, for he who doubts is like a wave of the sea driven and tossed by the wind. For let not that man suppose that he will receive anything from the Lord." It is not about begging God to do something; it is about believing that He not only will do it, but that He is waiting for you to come to Him so that He can do it. Everything that you do as a child of God hinges on your belief.

We must remember that even when the law of the Hebrews was in its fullness, that no one was ever saved because of it. Galatians 2:16 says, "knowing that a man is not justified by the works of the law but by faith in Jesus Christ, even we have believed in Christ Jesus, that we might be justified by faith in Christ and not by the works of the law; for by the works of the law no flesh shall be justified."

If we look in the book of Hebrews, the 11th chapter, we find that everything that we received from the Father we received because of faith. And faith can only come through what we believe.

Hebrews 11:1 tells us what faith is. It is the realization of what we hope for. It is the confidence to believe in something even when we can't see it. This chapter in Hebrews goes on to say that all the great men of the Bible were great, not because of what they did, but because of what they believed. So we must understand that the way faith and belief works has always been the same way from the beginning until now. Nothing has ever changed because of the law. So if you want to please God, you must do it by belief, which will become faith, and not by doing any work made by God or man. If you must work on something, work on your belief.

Belief is the most important thing you can do because if you don't believe, you won't accept. And if you don't accept, you will never have freedom. If you don't have freedom, you won't have peace. If you don't attain peace, you will not accept the righteousness of your Father. And without the righteousness given to you by your Father, you will try to obtain your own righteousness through some law or doctrine. And with that trying, you will fail. And with that failure, and will condemn yourself. And with that condemnation, your guilt will be more than you can bear. So you will convince yourself that God is mad at you, that He will not help you, that He only wants to judge you, and then, after He has judged you, that He cannot wait to punish you. So in all of your needs and wants in life, you will run as hard as you can *away* from your Father, when all He has ever wanted is for you to run *to* Him, to rest, and lie down in the peace and love that He provided for every single one of His children through the finished work of His Son Jesus.

It all starts with what you believe to be the truth about your Heavenly Father. It is up to you whether to knock on His door and accept all the wonderful gifts that He has for you. Or do you go on believing that He is not home, or even worse, that He does not desire a personal relationship with you, His beloved child?

8

Guard Your Heart

Very few children of God today understand the importance of the heart even though it is mentioned over 800 times in scripture, and most of these mentions of the heart refer to it as the center of who you are and what you will become. For through your heart, you will process everything that you experience in your life. And what you allow into your heart will ultimately determine who you will become. It is the center of every good thing and every bad thing that will happen in your life. Everything in your life that you truly believe will be processed through your heart.

If the heart is so important, then why are we not taught how to guard it? That is a very good question. And the only answer that I have is our lack of understanding of just how important the heart is. But hopefully, before this chapter is finished, you will have a greater understanding of the heart and the importance it plays in both your relationship with your Father and the way that you relate to the world and His child.

At the very least I hope that this chapter would make you think about your heart in a whole new way. And the best-case scenario would be one that you would not only learn how to guard your heart, but also to rewrite over all the damage done to your heart by both the world and religion so that only the good that the Father intended would enter into your heart, and that the bad would never have a place in your heart or in your life.

How do we guard our heart? Through the knowledge of God's Word and the peace it brings. It says it best in Philippians 4:7, "and the peace of God, which surpasses all understanding, will guard your hearts and minds through Christ Jesus." It is the peace of God that we use to guard our minds and our hearts. We must accept the fact that there is no animosity between us and God. And through this peace, we will not accept anything into our minds that might damage our hearts. We will only allow into our heart those things which we know to be the truth because we know the nature of our Father, so any and all lies about Him will be quickly expelled.

To put it another way, if you are secure in the knowledge that you are His child and that He is never mad at you, that He only wants what is best for you always, then, and only then, will you rest in the peace that was provided through the finished work of Jesus. And with that peace, your mind and your heart will be protected against the only thing the adversary has to harm you, his lies.

You must always keep in your heart the fact that since the new covenant of peace, there is only peace between you and your Heavenly Father. It is through this knowledge that your heart will be guarded. Knowledge is no more than learning about something. What are we trying to learn? We are trying to learn the nature of our Father. We must understand without a doubt that His nature is love and forgiveness, and that His love surpasses all understanding of this world. But until you understand this fact about His nature, you can never hope to rest in that peace, and your heart will continue to remain unguarded.

Everything that your mind perceives to be truth will eventually enter your heart. Whether that perception is right or wrong does not matter. Everything that you take into your mind as truth will have an opportunity to enter your heart. And that admission will shape the person you are now, as well as the person you will become in the future. Because of your perception of any given situation, whether truth or lie, your belief will always play a crucial part in changing your life to fit into what you believe. When that belief is written on your heart, it will shape your entire world. We will always allow both good and bad to enter into our hearts by what we believe.

Genesis 6:5 shows one of the first times that the thoughts of the heart are mentioned, both for man and God. "Then the Lord saw that the wickedness of man was great in the earth, and that every intent of the thoughts of his heart was only evil continually." This was the reason given by God for destroying man with a great flood. It is important to recognize that verse 6 says, "And the Lord was sorry that He had made man on the earth, and He was grieved in His heart."

There are many things to be learned about the nature of our Father from these writings. One of the most important lessons to be learned about His nature is the importance that the heart plays in our relationship with Him. The fact that we are still here as His children shows that His intent was always to have a relationship with His creation. He has always wanted nothing more than to have a loving relationship with His children.

If a person were to read a history of God's children with a subjective attitude, that person would wonder why the Creator of these children would not just scrap the whole project and start over. Two of the main proofs that our Father's nature is love and not judgment is: one, we are still here, and two, He sacrificed His only begotten Son to make this possible. As much as we would like to believe that this is all about us, it's not. It's about God the Father.

We must understand the truth about our Father, a truth that religion rarely teaches. We, as His children, have the ability to hurt Him with our actions, just as any child of a loving father can be hurt by his child's actions. The other thing to note is that God our Father felt the grief from His heart. As I have said, everything comes from the heart. If we want to understand just how closely we were created in the image of our Father, this would be a good place to start. Even the way we process knowledge into our hearts is the same way as God. Man processed knowledge and became evil in his heart. God processed the knowledge of what man was doing on the earth and became grieved in His heart.

It is clear that we were created so that the process of knowledge into the heart becomes belief, and this belief will always reside in the heart. This is the way God made us to function. If we can understand this process, we can control a vital part in maintaining our lives and our relationship with our Father.

Thoughts are talked about many places in scripture. Depending on the interpretation that is used, it could be interpreted as imagination, a plan, or an idea. But no matter how it is worded, the importance of what we let into our heart is the key to our relationship with God. This is vital to our happiness and peace here on earth.

The book of Proverbs is one of the best advice books ever written. It was written by a man with God-given wisdom. In almost every chapter of Proverbs the writer mentions the heart as a place where we do things from, or where we write things on. Proverbs 3:1–3 states, "My son, do not forget my law, But let your heart keep my commands; For length of days and long life And peace they will add to you. Let not mercy and truth forsake you; Bind them around your neck, Write them on the tablet of your heart." Verse 5 says "Trust in the Lord with all your heart." Verse 4:23 exhorts us, "Keep your heart with all diligence, For out of it spring the issues of life."

These verses plainly tell us that we need to keep our hearts safe, because our hearts are where we hold all that is precious and dear to us. Our hearts can be shaped and corrected. If you do not guard your heart and process what is allowed to enter into it, it will become perverse and wicked. And even more important than that, because we live out of our hearts, we too will become perverse and wicked.

It says in Proverbs 5:12, "How I have hated instruction, and my heart despised correction!" If you are to correct what is wrong in your life, the change will always begin through the heart.

Once you understand the importance of guarding your heart, the next question would be, how do I repair the damage that has been done to my heart? How do I keep my heart safe from any further damage? And how do I rewrite the wrong writings from a lifetime of writing on my heart?

The answer to these questions is to change what you really believe, or to repent. The religious people of today would have you believe that repentance is some superspiritual thing that happens when you run up to the altar in search of salvation. But if we were to break down the meaning of the word "repentance," you would find that the word simply means to change your mind. But this is the reason why repentance is so important to a child of God. If everything that you are is processed through the mind into the heart, it would stand to reason that to change your heart you must first change your mind. Even our first step toward salvation begins with the heart and what you truly believe. Romans 10:10 says, "For with the heart one believes unto righteousness, and with the mouth confession is made unto salvation." Whatever you have decided in your mind, you will ultimately write it on your heart, and this will be what you truly believe.

The Jewish people of Jesus' day were having trouble understanding this fact. They believed that a person had to do something more than believe to become righteous. Romans 10:2 says, "For I bear them witness that they have a zeal for God, but not according to knowledge." The Jews received the same message from the teaching of Jesus as everyone else. So the knowledge that they were lacking, spoken about in this verse, was not just information. It was the way they perceived or processed the information into their hearts that is spoken about here. It was because of a preconceived belief of the Jewish people that kept them from accepting who Jesus really was. Because of the information they had processed into their heart, they were blinded as to who the Messiah was. They believed because of the misinterpretation of their studies of God's Word that the Messiah would come as a conqueror. So when Jesus did not fit into their idea of what He should be, they rejected Him, because of what they had written on their hearts. And ultimately they tried to change the circumstances to fit what they believed to be true.

Romans 10:3 states, "For they being ignorant of God's righteousness, and seeking to establish their own righteousness, have not submitted to the righteousness of God." This is one of the main problems of the church today. They have a doctrine, or a preconceived idea, or knowledge, but remained ignorant of the truth, still trying to do something that they believe will make them righteous.

Now that we know how hard it is to change what is written on your heart, how do we keep from writing the wrong processed knowledge on our hearts? How do we write over the wrong and harmful things that are already in our hearts? Philippians 4:7 would provide the answer: "and the peace of God, which surpasses all understanding, will guard your hearts..." The answer is to filter everything you hear, feel, taste, touch, smell, and say through the Word of God, knowing that His nature is love and forgiveness not judgment, condemnation, or punishment, remembering always that because of His love, He sent His only begotten Son to fix the problem of sin.

Jesus has taken care of every wrong of the world through His finished work. That now, because of the new covenant of peace, the covenant that we now live in, there is no animosity between you and God. There is only peace. Realize that if you can accept this knowledge, that you will never let lies shape your heart. It is not necessary that you understand how this works. It is necessary, however, that you understand that it does work.

It is imperative that you understand that your only job, as a child of God, is to believe. You must understand it is not about what you can do, it is about what has already been done for you. You must come to realize that any time your thoughts and emotions are mixed with information or knowledge, it will write something on your heart. This can be good, but it can also be bad. If you perceive what the world is telling you, as a truth, it will usually be bad for your heart. This is why there are so many places in scripture that tell us that we are a new person and are not to be a part of this world and what it believes to be the truth.

Of course, you have to live in the world to accomplish the work that was given to you by Jesus. So those verses could only mean not to have the same heart as the world. And the only way you could accomplish this is by guarding what you allowed to enter into your heart. Then, and only then, can you have a heart for God and not for the world.

We must learn to recognize when something is being permanently written on our hearts. Ultimately, we are in control of what happens to our hearts. The proof in this statement is in each one of us. Think of something you believe to be a truth. Now think of the emotions that are related to the time when that truth became a fact in your life; the stronger the emotion the stronger the belief. Many things in our lives stimulate emotion, some we realize while it is happening. And some others, we have no idea why we are so emotional about a certain idea or belief.

One of the main tools used with our emotions is fear. An insurance company uses fear to sell insurance. If they can make you afraid of the future, then this emotion will cause you to write a new belief on your heart.

Another tool is music. Have you ever wondered why music is so important in the movies that we watch? Because without music, the makers of the movies could only rely on one sense, the sense of sight. The more senses that come into contact with the knowledge that we receive, the better the chances that we have of writing a new belief on our heart. There's absolutely nothing wrong with having all of your senses stimulated to the point of writing a new belief on your heart unless that belief is harmful to your life.

Religion is one of the best things at using your emotions to write things on your heart. And as I said, there is absolutely nothing wrong with this process, unless the information is flawed, because then, what you write on your heart will also be flawed.

I would love to say that everything the church teaches is correct. But if that were true, there would be no need for me to write this book. A large amount of the information that the churchgoing public has processing into their hearts every time they go to learn of God and His nature is flawed. And therefore, what the majority of God's children are writing on their hearts is also flawed. So in order to guard your heart, you must guard your emotions. You must learn to process the knowledge that your mind and emotions are receiving and only allow into your heart the information that was processed through the knowledge of God's Word and nature of God.

Control your feelings; recognize the manipulation used by the world. Stop any knowledge that would be harmful to your heart. Always process every piece of information through the understanding that you are a child of the Father who created everything. Second Corinthians 10:3–6 states, "For though we walk in the flesh, we do not war according to the flesh. For the weapons of our warfare are not carnal [of the flesh] but mighty in God for pulling down strongholds, casting down arguments [imagination] and every high thing that exalts itself against the knowledge of God, bringing every thought into captivity to the obedience of Christ, and being ready to punish all disobedience when your obedience is fulfilled." These verses state, without a doubt, exactly how things work for a child of God.

We do not fight the world with our bodies; our fight is in our mind. Our weapons are not external, but internal, given to us by our Father Himself. They were given to us for the purpose of tearing down mental strongholds, ideas, or anything that keeps us from the truth of God. These weapons are knowledge that we have received into our heart, such as salvation, righteousness, grace, peace, and the fact that we are adopted into a loving family of God.

Any attack by the world comes against not our bodies, but against our knowledge and our belief that we have written in our hearts, because as I have said many times in this chapter, you must always, without a doubt, know and understand who you really are. The way we fight against the attack on our knowledge and what we know to be truth is to take that thought into captivity. Stop each and every thought before it enters into your heart. Examine it, the way that Jesus did, through the filter of love and forgiveness, and the knowledge of your Father's nature. And after examining the thoughts for what they are, if they do not pass through the filter of God's love and the sacrifice of Jesus and all that He gave to us by His finished work, they will be abolished or done away with, never to gain entry into your heart. And therefore, never to cause you one moment of pain, because you refuse to believe the lie presented to you by the adversary.

Always believe God's Word. It is the only thing on this earth that does not change. It is the only truth that you can count on. Always remember that our Father has already given us every good gift with the Gospel (Good News) of peace. If something does not feel like Good News in your thoughts and your emotions, then do not let it be written on your heart. If what you are hearing induces fear or dread, it is not a message from your Father. Your heart is under attack. But hopefully now you understand how to guard your heart.

9
Law! What Law?

There is a complete misconception of what we are to do about the law as children of God. I know that a statement such as that can be misleading. But it is very important that we understand that as a child of God we no longer live by the law, whether it is the Jewish Law of Moses or the law imposed by the doctrine of a church or some religious organization. Once again, our understanding comes down to what Jesus accomplished through His finished work. If you do not understand everything that Jesus did while He was here on earth, then you will tend to misunderstand Matthew 5:17: "Do not think that I come to destroy the Law or the Prophets. I did not come to destroy but to fulfill." Jesus is telling the people that there appears to be a misunderstanding about what He was here to do. There was a misunderstanding about the way He was going to set God's children free. The same is true about our perception of scripture today. Because of wrong teaching and the misuse of scripture, God's children have a misunderstanding and have been led to believe something completely different than the truth. And with this wrong teaching, the children of God are still having as much trouble accepting the truth today as the children of Israel did in days gone by.

In verse 17, Jesus makes it very clear that He did not come to destroy the law. We've been taught that because it was not destroyed, it must still be applicable. Once again, man has taken a piece of the Word and not the whole Word to heart. We failed to realize that when an obligation is fulfilled, it is done away with. It is just as gone as if it had been destroyed. The difference is the reason why it is no longer here. If Jesus had destroyed the law as a means to get rid of it that would have indicated there something was wrong with the law. The only problem that existed with the law was man. Yet, the law had to be done away with for man to have a loving relationship with his Father.

Jesus came to fulfill the law, which, up until He had come, was only appeased by the blood of animals. It was not fulfilled. Matthew 5:18, if not taken in the proper context, will strengthen the wrong teaching of religion when it says, "For assuredly, I say to you, till heaven and earth pass away, one jot [the smallest letter] or one tittle [the smallest stroke in a Hebrew letter] will by no means pass from the law till all is fulfilled."

To understand what these verses mean, we only need to go to one word used in both: "fulfilled." Jesus is telling us in verse 17 that He came to fulfill the law. He states in verse 18 that without Him doing what He needed to do to fulfill the law that nothing would change.

The question we must ask ourselves is this. Did Jesus do what He said He would do? Because if He did, then the law is fulfilled. Matthew 5:20 says, "For I say to you, that unless your righteousness exceeds the righteousness of the scribes and the Pharisees, you will by no means enter the kingdom of heaven." Jesus is explaining to the people that even the religious leaders did not, and could not, obtain the righteousness required to gain entry into heaven by their own works through the law. The only way into heaven, according to this verse, is by righteousness. But more and better righteousness than could be attained by works of the law.

Romans 3:20 states, "Therefore by the deeds of the law no flesh will be justified [or made righteous] in His sight, for by the law is the knowledge of sin." As long as you live by a law, any law, you will always try to fix yourself as a means to attain righteousness. But you can never do enough to attain righteousness on your own, because you still think of yourself as a sinner. You must understand in your mind and in your heart that there is nothing you can do to attain the righteousness that is needed to have a relationship with your Father and to enter into the kingdom of heaven.

Romans 3:21–24 is the exact proof of this statement. "But now the righteousness of God apart from the law is revealed, being witnessed by the Law and the Prophets, even the righteousness of God, through faith in Jesus Christ, to all and on all who believe. For there is no difference; for all have sinned and fall short of the glory of God, being justified [made righteous] freely [without any cost] by His grace through the redemption that is in Christ Jesus."

The righteousness of God that is now yours has been paid for by Jesus. It is free to everyone who desires it. The only requirements you have on your part to take possession of righteousness is to believe. Righteousness through belief was not a new concept. The only righteousness ever attained in the history of man was attained through belief, not works.

Romans 4:4–5 says, "Now to him who works, the wages are not counted as grace but as debt. But to him who does not work but believes on Him who justifies [or makes righteous] the ungodly, his faith is accounted for righteousness." If you read the rest of Romans 4, you will see that it was because of faith that Abraham was called righteous. It was not because of works.

In Hebrews 11, we see the list of great men of the Bible. We see very clearly that everything that they did meant nothing next to their faith. That everything that was accounted to them was because of faith. As it says in Hebrews 11:6, "But without faith it is impossible to please Him, for he who comes to God must believe that He is, and that He is a rewarder of those who diligently seek Him."

We must first believe in the Father, and then sincerely want to have a relationship with Him. And with this relationship, you will begin to understand about all the wonderful gifts that have been provided to you, by God, through the finished work of His Son Jesus. We understand through belief in the finished work of Jesus comes faith, and through faith you are now accounted with the righteousness of God. What do you have to do for all the good gifts of God? Simply believe! James 1:17 informs us, "Every good gift and every perfect gift is from above, and comes down from the Father of lights, with whom there is no variation or shadow of turning."

Now with a clear understanding that we, as God's children, have no need for the law any longer, I am compelled to tell you that if you continue to sin, your life will not change for the better. The apostle Paul tells us in Corinthians that the unrighteous will not inherit the kingdom of God. But after a long list explaining what kind of sinners they were, the next verses tell them that they are not those people anymore. Because they were set apart, or sanctified, by the blood of Jesus and by the Spirit of God the Father Himself, that because of these gifts, they are a different kind of creature now.

Paul says in 1 Corinthians 6:12, "All things are lawful for me, but all things are not helpful. All things are lawful for me, but I will not be brought under the power of any." Paul is saying in this verse that he does not live by the law, any law. The reason he does not do the things he listed in the paragraphs that preceded this one is because of the destruction it would bring into his life. He says that anything that does not help in his life is a hindrance and that he will not give it any power over his life. I am sorry to say, this is not superspiritual or ultrareligious, this is just plain old common sense. Make no mistake; what you allow to have power over your life will ultimately affect you and the people around you.

James 1:13–15 tells believers, "Let no one say when he is tempted, 'I am tempted by God'; for God cannot be tempted by evil, nor does He Himself tempt anyone. But each one is tempted when he is drawn away by his own desires and enticed. Then when desire has conceived, it gives birth to sin; and sin, when it is full-grown, brings forth death."

Never think that because you no longer live by the law that you are immune to the effects of sowing and reaping. The seeds that you plant in your life you will reap as a harvest of good or bad, depending on the seed you sow. But the important thing in this verse is that we must be willing to be drawn away from our Father and the relationship that we have with Him before any sin can happen. So always watch for the beginning of sin. Pay attention to the distance you are from the Father, at any given moment. Remember, sin does not "just happen."

To reach a point of sin in your life is to take a path of progression that goes like this. First, you let go of your Father's hand because of something that entices you that you desire to have. At this point, you realize that you are getting farther away from your Father. You have a choice then, to go after what you desire or to turn back and take hold of your Father's hand once again. Now, if you choose not to go back to the Father, this is your choice. You must realize, nothing has changed in your relationship with your Father other than the fact that you are wandering about on your own. But if your desire has overtaken you and has become a thought or feeling that you have turned into an action and now that you have acted upon this desire to move away from God, it is the beginning of sin. It is still not too late to turn around and take hold of your Father's hand. But if you still choose not to, then you are in the last steps of your journey to sin. The sin is now grown in size and strength, and if you still choose not to take hold of your Father's hand, then the seed that you have planted is yours to reap.

But even now with all the strength that you have given this sin that has a hold on you, it has no strength when you compare it to the power of your Father and the power of Jesus Christ, your friend and savior. It can do nothing to you except what you allow it to do, because that same spirit which raised Jesus from the dead dwells in you.

First John 1:9 says, "If we confess our sins, He is faithful and just to forgive us our sins and to cleanse us from all unrighteousness." Remember that to repent is nothing more than to change your mind. In order to get out of sin, you must simply change your mind and decide to take God's hand. He was waiting at the beginning of your life, He has been there with you every step you take in your life, and He will be there always watching, always ready for you to raise your hand toward Him so that He might take hold of His precious child and lead him or her out of their self-inflicted pain caused by a false desire to have something they did not need in the first place.

First Corinthians 15:56–57 says, "The sting of death is sin, and the strength of sin is the law. But thanks be to God, who gives us the victory through our Lord Jesus Christ." It is my hope that now you would understand that because of Jesus you are the righteousness of God, that both sin and death hold no power over you any longer.

Hebrews 7:18–19 explains, "For on the one hand there is an annulling of the former commandment because of its weakness and unprofitableness, for the law made nothing perfect [complete]; on the other hand, there is the bringing in of a better hope, through which we draw near to God." It simply means that the law didn't work for man. But now we are able to have a relationship with our Father, the kind of relationship that He has always wanted with His children. He fixed everything with the new covenant so we could not mess it up, no matter how hard we try. The only thing that we have to do is go to Him and be at peace because of love, not law.

First Corinthians 14:33 says, "For God is not the author of confusion but of peace, as in all the churches of the saints." God did not make His Word confusing; man did. If you are having a hard time understanding what you are supposed to do, always go back to the relationship with your Father, because with this relationship, you will begin to understand His nature. And in knowing His nature, you will understand that it is not hard to be His child. It's not about rules; it is about a relationship. It is not about a religion; it is about a relationship. Do everything you do from this point on, out of love, not obligation. This is the first step to acting like a son or daughter of God.

God did what He did for you out of love not obligation. Jesus did what He did for you out of love not obligation. Now you go and do what you do for God your Father and Jesus your friend and brother out of love not obligation.

10
Righteousness Is a Gift

Like almost everything else that God has provided to His children through the finished work of Jesus, organized religion has misunderstood, misconstrued, and generally missed the importance of understanding righteousness. One of the most important gifts that were given to us after our salvation is His righteousness. But I find that like most of the gifts of the Father, it too remains unavailable because His children refused to accept it as a gift.

Most churches today teach that righteousness is something you must be good enough to receive. You must work hard enough and long enough to put on the righteousness of the Father. Almost as if it were something unattainable by anyone but the super-religious or the ultraspiritual, when, in fact, if you believe, then you are saved. If you are saved, then you are a child of God. If you are a child of God, then you are righteous. If you are righteous, then your righteousness could have only come from one source, from your Father Himself. You are the righteousness of God Himself.

I know what you're thinking, especially if you were taught with the misunderstanding of most church doctrines. You are thinking, *I had better put this book down; it's going to start saying things like I'm righteous.* That's blasphemy to say that you are the righteousness of God. But I did not say it. Scripture says this. Romans 3:21 and 22 are quite clear. They say, "But now the righteousness of God apart from the law is revealed, being witnessed by the Law and the

Prophets, even the righteousness of God, through faith in Jesus Christ, to all and on all who believe. For there is no difference;"

These words given to God's children plainly tell us two things. One, we are righteous, and two, our righteousness comes from God. The problem is that, like most of the gifts that the Father has provided for His children, there must be an understanding, and then an acceptance, before the gift can be utilized to its full potential.

From this point forward, we will consider everything that God has given us as a free gift, because this is the first part of understanding who you are. Any gift that is given to you by your Father is free. It is given because of the great and wonderful love of the Giver. You do not need to do anything but receive the gift and acknowledge the contents. It is free to you.

The only thing you need to do is take it and open it, and then keep it for your very own. You did not just get the gift of salvation when you became a child of God. You received many wonderful and glorious gifts from your Father at that moment.

Because of the finished work of Jesus Christ our Lord and Savior, the Father was able to bestow all these gifts to His children. But just like any other gift, if you refuse to take it, if you refuse to open it, if you refuse to accept it as your very own, then the gift remains useless to you. And I'm sorry to say that once again, because of your choice, you are not living the kind of life that your Father intended for you to live.

What is needed now is for you to accept the gifts of your Father. And with the acceptance of the gifts, you have a realization that will establish you in His righteousness.

How can I be so bold as to keep saying that we have the righteousness of God? Because that is exactly what 2 Corinthians 5:21 says. "For He made Him who knew no sin to be sin for us, that we might become the righteousness of God in Him." You can in no way misread this verse. You are not only righteous, but there was a trade between you and your Savior Jesus. You did not negotiate the trade. Your Father negotiated the trade so that there was no way that you could lose. Your Father made sure that you would come out on top. The only thing you have to do in this trade is to reach in your pocket and pull out that nasty wad of black slime known as sin and give it to Jesus. And Jesus will pull out God's righteousness and trade it with you.

When you make this trade, there is something very important that happens. You now have in your possession the righteousness of God. You no longer have any sin in your possession. You just made a trade with Jesus and gave all your sin that you had to Him.

But because it is such a good trade on your part, you will keep trying to add something else to it. You will try to appease that thought that you have that you might have cheated Jesus. You must realize that the reason for the trade had nothing to do with your worth or what you wanted. You must realize that the agreement was made between Jesus and our Father, not between our Father and you. And because of what Jesus did, it was possible now for your Father to have that same kind of relationship with you, and the rest of His children that He has with Jesus. That the trade Jesus made on the cross of Calvary was made for every person, and that it was made forever. The righteousness of God is yours to keep forever, and the sin that you traded for that righteousness is gone forever.

But in order for righteousness to work, you must accept the gift or become established in your belief. Why is it so important that we accept this fact of the gift of righteousness? Because we have been taught that if you are not righteous you can not get into heaven. One of the main doctrines of religion teaches that you must work to attain enough righteousness to win that place as a son of God.

Romans 1:16–17 states, "For I am not ashamed of the gospel [good news] of Christ, for it is the power of God to salvation for everyone who believes, for the Jew first and also for the Greek. For in it [the Gospel] the righteousness of God is revealed from faith to faith; as it is written, 'The just [righteous] shall live by faith.'" If you break down these two versus you will expel the myth of most church doctrines about righteousness.

Let's begin where Paul began, with the main power of the Gospel. There are four important things we need to examine about the power of the Gospel. First, it is God Himself who supplies the power of the Gospel. Second, it is for every person on earth. Third, the Gospel (Good News) is a God-given power to salvation. And fourth, the only way to tap into that God-given power is to believe the truth of the Gospel, or Good News.

Verse 17 finishes this statement about not only the Gospel but also where your righteousness comes from. It informs believers that in it ("it" being the Gospel) God's righteousness is revealed.

It is very important that we believe how God's righteousness in us came to be. We must ask ourselves, how is God's righteousness revealed? The answer is through the Good News of the Gospel you believe, and with your belief there is an acceptance of God's power in you. Without the gift of God's righteousness in you, you cannot be saved. But with it, you are absolutely and without a doubt a saved child of God.

The last part of this verse is very important. It sums up why the church doctrine is so wrong in thinking we must do work to attain our righteousness. It says that the righteousness in us is revealed from "faith to faith." It does not say that righteousness is revealed in us from faith to works. This statement by Paul clearly says that from the beginning of righteousness to the end of righteousness, it only has to do with faith in the Father, through His power, brought on by belief in the Good News that Jesus finished God's work here on earth. In the last line of this verse we expel every other way of thinking when it says, "The just [or righteous] shall live by faith," not by works.

The acceptance of the gift of righteousness has always been a problem for religion. Even the first-generation church was having problems with the fact that it is a free gift. Romans 9 and 10 states that one of the main reasons that Israel could not be saved is because they stumbled on the fact of what Jesus did to eliminate sin on the earth. They did not understand that it was for God's benefit as well as for ours. Because without the work that Jesus did, His Father could not have a relationship with the rest of His children. The Jewish people could not let go of the idea of salvation by works.

Oddly enough, most Christians I know were never Jews. So it fascinates me when I see them trying to act like Jews where the law is concerned. Consider Romans 9:30–32, "What shall we say then? That Gentiles, who did not pursue righteousness, have attained to righteousness, even the righteousness of faith; but Israel, pursuing the law of righteousness, has not attained to the law of righteousness. Why? Because they did not seek it by faith, but as it were, by the works of the law. For they stumbled at that stumbling stone." These verses tell us that the reason that Israel could not attain righteousness is because they were using works and not faith.

Any time you or your church find yourself trying to do something to attain righteousness, you are caught in the same "works-righteousness mentality" that Paul tried so hard to expel in his letters. According to everything that the apostle Paul wrote, righteousness cannot be attained by something that you can physically do. Righteousness can only be attained through faith in your Father, and faith in your Lord Jesus.

If you study the Bible at all, you might ask yourself, "Doesn't it say in the book of James that you are to be 'doers of the word'"? Absolutely! This verse is as valid and true as any verse in the Bible.

The difference between my statement and the statements of most of the religious doctrines is the reason why you are a doer of the Word. Once you realize all the wonderful gifts that you now possess because of the finished work of our Lord Jesus, you cannot help but to be a doer of God's Word, for the simple fact that with the realization of who you are now and what you have been given you will not only become a son of God, but you will act like a son of God. But in spite of what religion teaches, this is done through the acceptance of the gifts, through the knowledge of righteousness, grace, and peace with the Father, and the acceptance of whom you are and why it is imperative for your transformation out of the world and into God's family. In essence, you become the person through the gifts of your Father that the church teaches that you become through works.

The fallacy of the religious teachings of today is that there is no power at work in your life other than the power that you, yourself, are able to muster. At the very moment that you make a decision to believe in the teachings of Jesus Christ and all that He did for you, at that very second that you accept the gifts of God, you become an adopted son or daughter and God's grace immediately begins the transformation from the vagabond you were, to the prince or princess that you are now.

Scripture states in Romans 10:2–4 that you can be on fire for God. You can go to church every time the doors open. You can give everything you feel that you should give, every time you feel it. You can stand up and volunteer every time the church asks for help. But all of these things will get you nothing and lead you nowhere if you don't receive the knowledge and understanding that God's righteousness is a free gift. The only way anyone can hope to attain this wonderful gift is to submit to the knowledge and belief that it is yours because of the finished work of Jesus.

Romans 10:2–4 says, "For I bear them witness that they [Israel] have a zeal for God, but not according to knowledge. For they being ignorant of God's righteousness, and seeking to establish their own righteousness, have not submitted to the righteousness of God. For Christ is the end of the law for righteousness to everyone who believes." Take this free gift from your Father and wear it proudly because it is only given to His children out of His unfailing love. Go and tell the world who you are and that you are saved from sin and so much more. Show them what a son and daughter of God looks like. And let them know without a doubt that it was a gift attained through *belief*, and not any type of works.

Romans 10:10 states, "For with the heart one believes unto righteousness, and with the mouth confession is made unto salvation." If it sounds easy, it is, because our Father knows that His children will mess anything up if it is too complicated. Understand and believe who you really are now because of Jesus. When you truly believe with all your heart, every single molecule in your world will start to take shape in that direction, in the direction that a son of God would take, instead of a defeated child of the world; from the view point of belief you will become the kind of person you were always meant to be. But first, you must give up the idea that you are trying to do something to attain it on your own. Just stop and receive the wonderful gifts of God. Open them, hug your Father's neck, and thank Him.

11

Adopted into the Family

As I am sure you realize by now, the main problem that God's children have in utilizing the gifts that He has provided for us is in the simple recognition of who we really are and who we are to become after the adoption into our Heavenly Father's family, and that we accept and use His gifts. As it is in most things in life, truth is only truth if we accept it as fact. Once you have accepted truth as fact, then it will become your truth, whether the facts are valid or invalid.

For example, the ancient world and what they relied on as fact teaches us a lot about misconception and how it can alter the perception of the world. For instance, at one time, the scientific world believed that the world was flat, and that the earth was the center of the universe. At the time that these theories came into existence, the religious world embraced them with such vigor that they made it heresy for anyone to speak differently. Now we know that the world is not flat, and that the earth is not the center of the universe. But even with this knowledge, if the scientific and religious ideology of truth had not been altered, then the real truth could have caused us to be put to death for heresy.

We understand through this example that truth does not need to have a basis of fact to become truth. It simply needs to have a basis of what the majority believes to be true to become truth. The problems with this way of thinking are obvious, because when mankind believed the world to be flat, then man was afraid to journey beyond the horizon. Because of what he believed to be true, he was inhibited, not able to reach his full potential because of fear.

Today when we look at the whole concept of a flat world, we think that mankind was very silly to believe such lies. We say to ourselves, "I would never be so silly as to think the world was flat." "I would never allow an unproven idea or a lie to paralyze me." "Our scientists and religious leaders today are too smart to let that happen to us." "They are too advanced to have any of the same type of misconceptions that might lead to a misunderstanding of the way everything works." We know everything about everything, don't we?

The fact is that God's children have been paralyzed in much the same way as the ancient world. The untruths and misconceptions that they choose to believe today have no more validity than the lies of the ancient world. The only reason that the children of God are where they are today, the only reason the world is in the shape it is in today, is that we have accepted as truth the misconception of who our Father is, what His Word means, and who we are in perspective to everything around us.

God's children have, without a doubt, been misled in the respect of who they are and the power they have been given. They have been led to believe that they are less than they are. In explaining the way that this particular concept works, I would like to go to a movie that I saw as a child, *The Prince and the Pauper*. This is a movie that I saw in school long before Beta or VHS. Yes, it was shown from a projector against the wall of my classroom.

The reason I bring this movie up is because as I began to realize how the gifts of God worked, this movie kept coming to mind. Now for those of you who have not seen the Disney film *The Prince and the Pauper*, I will recap it for you. There was a prince, of course, who lived in a castle, protected from the outside world. And as it is human nature, his every thought was to get outside the castle walls and explore the world around him. Also in this story was a poor boy, or a pauper. Now the poor boy, being born on the streets and living in poverty, would always look at the castle with dreams of being safe in its walls and having all the wonderful benefits that the prince must surely have. And as fate would have it, one day, the poor boy snuck into the castle grounds with the intention of stealing something of value, or at least to find something to eat.

Naturally, the prince and the poor boy would meet on this day and realize that they were identical twins. So they concocted a plan to switch places for the day. And they did. The prince took on the role of a vagabond, and the poor boy took on the role as a prince. The only problem with this plan was that they could not switch back when the time came. The prince was destined to live on the streets for a time. And the poor boy was destined to take the role of a prince for that same time.

Now the interesting part of this story is what happens to the two young men while they are in this role reversal. The prince is now forced to act like a poor street urchin. And so he turns to stealing and lying and cheating because this is the role he was cast in. And the pauper is forced to act like a prince in order to not give away the deception that he is really just a pauper.

Interestingly, the longer that each of the two young men act in the role that they are playing, the more they become those people that they are forced to act like.

The story of God's children is very similar to this in a way. What we accept as fact will determine what we do and how we will live as that child. Who we choose to listen to about who we are will determine who we will ultimately become. If we accept the role of a prince, as the poor boy did, then we will choose to act like a prince, and ultimately become one. If you accept the fact that you are now an adopted child of God and accept the fact that you now have all the power and authority that a child of God should have, then you are a prince working in the power of your Father.

However, if you choose to believe that you are a pauper, then you will also believe that there is no power or authority in your life. You will become a prince that acts like a pauper. The greatest problem with this way of thinking is you will tend to blame your Heavenly Father for your poor choices. You will come to believe the lies of the adversary, who has always hated us and the Father. You will believe that you are nothing and that you have no power. This is the biggest lie that has ever been told to mankind. Ultimately, the decision is yours, whether to believe that you are a prince or that you are a pauper.

In order to keep from making the wrong decision about what the facts are, we must become secure in who we really are. If we will thoroughly understand that we are the adopted children of the one God who created everything, then, and only then, can we fight the lies that are told to us. In order to fully understand who we are now, we must first accept that we are no longer what we were. We cannot thoroughly take hold of something in our lives if our lives are full of something else. The first thing that we must do is to convince ourselves to let go of who we were so that there will be room to accept who we are. We need to understand that because we are a new person that the change in you will come, if you let it. We need to understand that it is because of all the gifts that God has provided that we are different.

But if you do not accept the gifts, opening and using each one, they will not work. You cannot change your life on your own without accepting who you are. You must ultimately accept all the wonderful gifts that the Father has provided to make this transition possible.

The beginning of this change starts with the knowledge that you are a child of God. The definition of the Greek word for *knowledge* means, a "recognition, discernment, or acknowledgment." We can understand from this definition you need to recognize and acknowledge both who you are and all of the gifts from God that you have attained.

The apostle Paul explains it to the Colossians this way. He says that the reason that they do not need to lie is because they are a new man because of the gifts of God brought by the finished work of Jesus. Colossians 3:9–10 says, "Do not lie to one another, since you have put off the old man with his deeds, and have put on a new man who is renewed in the knowledge according to the image of Him who created him."

Ephesians 4:13 informs us, "till we all come to the unity of the faith and of the knowledge of the Son of God, to a perfect man, to the measure of the stature of the fullness of Christ." Second Peter 1:2–4 says, "Grace and peace be multiplied to you in the knowledge of God and of Jesus our Lord, as His divine power has given to us all things that pertain to life and godliness, through the knowledge of Him who called us by glory and virtue, by which have been given to us exceedingly great and precious promises, that through these you may be partakers of the divine nature, having escaped the corruption that is in the world through lust."

These verses above plainly tell us that when you completely accept, recognize, discern, and acknowledge the truth, that you are a child of the King and that at that moment a transformation will begin to take place in you. We have been given "everything that pertains to life and godliness." It does not say, if you can work hard enough or give enough money, or be good enough, that you will receive the gifts for a wonderful life. No! It says you have been given all things for a wonderful life, for a godly life, just as a prince of God should have. You have been given everything you need for the transformation into that changed person that is spoken about in these versus. You are now, because of God's grace and God's righteousness, a godly person that you were always intended to be.

It is through the knowledge (to accept, discern, and acknowledge) of who you are now and why you are different now, that you can enter a relationship with your Father. It is not something done by you. You cannot do anything apart from accepting and believing in Jesus and what He accomplished for you.

First John 2:23 states, "Whoever denies the Son does not have the Father either; he who acknowledges the Son has the Father also." First John 3:1 says, "Behold what manner of love the Father has bestowed on us, that we should be called children of God!" It is only because of the unsurpassed love of God that we are able to have the status of His children.

"Every good gift and every perfect gift is from above, and comes down from the Father of lights, with whom there is no variation or shadow of turning" (James 1:17). Every good and perfect gift that has been given to man from the time that Jesus went to be with the Father is still here for His children today. There is "no variation or shadow of turning" with our Father. First Thessalonians 5:5 says, "You are all sons of light and sons of the day. We are not of the night nor of darkness." Ephesians 5:8 proclaims, "For you were once darkness, but now you are light in the Lord. Walk as children of light."

Our Father only gives us the best that He has to give. If you are not receiving the best, it is not from your Father, it is from the world. Get out of the world! Or for a more accurate statement, get the world out of you! Because when you expel all of the lies that the world has told you about love, happiness, fulfillment, and peace, there will be an abundance of room for the gifts provided by your Father.

As we are instructed in Colossians 3:2, you must change the way you perceive the world around you. You must "Set your mind on things above, not on things on the earth." Then, and only then, will you come to realize that you are an adopted son or daughter of the Heavenly Father.

Ephesians 1:5 states, "having predestined us to adoption as sons by Jesus Christ to Himself, according to the good pleasure of His will." And with this understanding, you will be able to utilize every gift provided by your Father. Colossians 1:12 encourages us, "giving thanks to the Father who has qualified us to be partakers of the inheritance of the saints in the light." "You are all sons of light and sons of day. We are not of the night nor of the darkness" (1 Thessalonians 5:5). Start today!

Open the gifts provided by your Father. Open the gifts of an abundant life that He has always intended for His children to live. Remember the words in John 10:10, "The thief does not come except to steal, and to kill, and to destroy. I have come that they may have life, and that they may have it more abundantly."

Because Jesus came to be the last sacrifice ever needed on earth or in heaven, we, as God's children, can have that loving, wonderful relationship with our Father, just as Jesus does. It is okay to crawl up in His lap, hug His neck, and say thank you, Abba [Daddy]. And while you are there telling Him how much you love Him, let Him show you just how much He has always loved you.

12
Recognizing the Gospel

When understanding the nature of our Father, it is important that we understand how to recognize what the Gospel of Christ really is. Not what it has been distorted into. Going into this chapter, the first and most important thing we need to know is what the simple, but accurate definition of the word *Gospel* is. It means "Good News." This is something that the religious world of today seems to forget.

I have listened to countless teachings from various religious organizations, and their gospel was anything but Good News. So for that reason as we enter into this chapter, I would ask that you would keep this definition in the forefront of your mind. That the Gospel of Christ is nothing but Good News. Let us use this definition from this moment on to determine if it is, in fact, the Gospel of Christ Jesus that we are being taught. And if we filter all of our thinking through this definition, it should be easy to distinguish if we are being deceived with the teaching that we are receiving. Because if we are listening to the teaching that refers to judgment, condemnation, and prejudice, then we are not listening to the true Gospel, the Gospel that Jesus told us, as His disciples, to go and tell the whole world about.

This is not a new problem. In fact, most of the letters written in the New Testament of the Bible were written because someone was not teaching the first-century church the true Gospel. Instead, they were trying to refine and misinterpret the Gospel that Jesus gave them, and us. It is a sad fact that this problem has carried over into today's church.

What is the Good News of the Gospel of Jesus? Our first clue that was given to man about the Good News of Christ is in a story that almost everyone is familiar with. Every Christmas we hear about how the angels came and told the shepherds that they should not fear because they bring good news to all the people of the world. Recall in Luke 2:10, "Then the angel said to them, 'Do not be afraid, for behold, I bring you good tidings of great joy which will be to all people.'"

You might say to yourself, okay, I see that we have good news, but what is the good news? The angel goes on to tell the shepherds that a Savior has come to save all of mankind. What is the Savior saving mankind from? Sin! And so much more will be done for man because of His coming. The Good News is that because of our Savior and His provision for our salvation from sin, we now have been reinstated into God's family, with all the gifts, rights, and privileges due a son of God. Also that God is our Father, and He will never be mad at us again because of the work that Jesus did.

Isaiah 52–54 tells us of all the things that God is going to do with the finished work of Jesus. It says that God had a plan to fix the problem of sin. Then it goes on to tell how He intends to do this very important task. We must realize that at the time that God said this, He had not yet accomplished everything that is written in these verses. But now it has been completed by Jesus. When we read about the promises of the Father that were made before Jesus had finished the work that our Father had given Him to do, it is important to remember that now they are valid because Jesus has come to the earth for that very purpose.

When it says in Isaiah 54:9–10, "For this is like the waters of Noah to Me; For as I have sworn that the waters of Noah would no longer cover the earth, so have I sworn that I would not be angry with you, nor rebuke you. For the mountains shall depart, and the hills be removed, but My kindness shall not depart from you, nor shall My covenant of peace be removed." God, your Father, gave His Word that He would never be mad at us again. That with the finished work of Jesus, we would be at peace with our Father forever. Still, there are many doctrines and teachings that came along after Jesus completed His works that are incorrect according to this promise made by God.

As I have said before, a wrong teaching of the Gospel is nothing new; it has been around almost as long as the true Gospel itself. Titus 1:10–11 states, "For there are many insubordinate, both idle talkers and deceivers, especially those of the circumcision, whose mouths must be stopped, who subvert whole households, teaching things which they ought not, for the sake of dishonest gain." Everything that was going on in the above verses that caused a man of God to write this letter is *still* going on today. There are people today that are trying to make a dishonest gain from the Good News of the Gospel. What we must realize is this: the Gospel is free to every person on this planet. It is free to us, because it was paid for by Jesus. If at any time you hear that you have to pay to receive the Good News, in any way, shape, or form, then it is not the Gospel of Jesus Christ that you are hearing.

Another problem that we have with understanding the Good News of the Gospel is the problem of people adding things to it and claiming it is still the Gospel of Jesus Christ. Galatians 1:6–7 says, "I marvel that you are turning away so soon from Him who called you in the grace of Christ, to a different gospel, which is not another; but there are some who trouble you and want to pervert [distort] the gospel of Christ." Almost every teaching that is different from the true Gospel removes the power of grace and returned to some form of works. My friend, this doctrine will never be the Gospel. Any gospel that substitutes grace for works is not the Gospel of Jesus Christ.

It is important to tell you that just because a church is not teaching the true Gospel it does not mean that they do not have good intentions. Most of the time they do not see or understand what is wrong in what they are doing. They feel that their doctrine or teachings are the right way, and they are sincere in their love, both to God and His children. The problem is that they are confused, and no matter how good their intentions are, a confused person cannot lead another lost person out of the darkness. But if it is any consolation, realize that even the apostle Peter messed up the Gospel, trying to combine its Jewish beliefs with the teachings of Christ Jesus. And the apostle Paul had to remind him of who he was also.

Galatians 2:11–16 states, "Now when Peter had come to Antioch, I withstood him to his face, because he was to be blamed; for before certain men came from James, he would eat with the Gentiles; but when they came, he withdrew and separated himself, fearing those who were of the circumcision. And the rest of the Jews also played the hypocrite with him, so that even Barnabas was carried away with their hypocrisy. But when I saw that they were not straightforward about the truth of the gospel, I said to Peter before them all, 'If you, being a Jew, live in this manner of Gentiles and not as the Jews, why do you compel Gentiles to live as Jews? We who are Jews by nature, and not sinners of the Gentiles, knowing that a man is not justified [made righteous] by the works of the law but by faith in Jesus Christ, even we have belief in Christ Jesus, that we might be justified by faith in Christ and not by the works of the law; for by the works of the law no flesh shall be justified.'" Even Peter messed up.

It does not mean that Peter was a bad guy. It just means that he messed up. What we need to learn from these verses is that everyone is capable of messing up the Gospel. This just simply means that we need to pay very close attention to the teachings that we are receiving. No matter who the teacher is or how established any particular organized religion might be, we still need to make sure they are teaching the truth. Do not be mad or judge when you realize that you have been taught the wrong gospel. Some of these wrong teachings have been around almost as long as the true Gospel.

How can we tell if it is the one true Gospel of Christ Jesus? This can only be done through knowledge of your Father and His nature, and the knowledge of His Word. As I have said before, with these two things you cannot be lied to, and when all of the lies are expelled, then only truth remains, and when only the truth remains, then you will see the Gospel of Jesus.

Because of the realization of who the Father is and why He has done what He has done, you will refuse to listen to anything that goes against this understanding. Through a clearer understanding of His Word, you will come to accept your position as His child. With His Spirit to guide you, the truth of the

Good News of the Gospel will be more than apparent to you.

First John 2:27 states, "But the anointing which you have received from Him abides in you, and you do not need that anyone teach you; but as the same anointing teaches you concerning all things, and is true, and is not a lie, and just as it is taught you, you will abide in Him." Once you know the truth about your Father, you will never want to leave Him because of the peace and love that you have with Him. The only way to know your Father is to establish a relationship with Him. And the only way to establish a relationship with anyone, including your Father, is to put in the time that it takes to know them.

Too many children of God think that they can have a relationship with their Father by going to church for two hours on Sunday and two hours on Wednesday. That does not make good sense by any definition. What if you were to put only four hours a week into the relationship with your wife or your children or your best friend? What kind of a relationship would that be? The same is true with our relationship with our Father. The majority of churchgoing Christians spend more time on their favorite sport than with their Father. The majority of them can quote statistics about who, what, when, where, and how their favorite team is doing, but very few of them actually know their Father and what His Word truly says or means. Then these same people fail to understand why they are so lost when it comes to spiritual matters.

There is an old saying that goes: "You will get out of life what you put into it." This is true, and God is life. Put more in the relationship with your Father and you will always get more out of it.

You can only know the Gospel of Jesus if you are a disciple of Jesus. To be a disciple means simply that you will follow the teachings of the person you want to be a disciple of. Many Christians claim to be a disciple and have no idea what Jesus' teachings are, much less follow His teachings. There are a lot of teachings out there that claim to be of Jesus. Upon examination, using scripture as a filter, there are a lot of teachings that are not even close to what Jesus taught. We have the Gospels of Matthew, Mark, Luke, John, and we also have Acts to tell us about Jesus and His teachings. An important thing to realize is not only what Jesus said in these writings, but just as important is how He acted and reacted to God the Father and His children. Jesus said if you see Him, you see the Father.

John 5:19–20 tells us, "Then Jesus answered and said to them, 'Most assuredly, I say to you, the Son can do nothing of Himself, but what He sees the Father do; for whatever He does, the Son also does in like manner. For the Father loves the Son, and shows Him all things that He Himself does; and He will show Him greater works than these, that you will marvel.'"

A couple of very important facts that we need to understand in these versus are that Jesus admitted that He did nothing on His own. That God showed Jesus His nature and that was the guideline for His work. And also that God the Father did this because of His love for Jesus, His Son. After understanding these two facts we must realize that we also see God's nature, because Jesus lives in us. We also see God's nature, because the same Spirit that was revealing God's nature to Jesus is in us. So the revelation that Jesus had because of God's Spirit, we also have. When we establish that same kind of relationship with our Father that Jesus had, we allow ourselves, through His Spirit, to know His nature.

Just as Jesus is loved by our Father, we are His beloved children also. So we can understand from these verses that every reason that Jesus gives for knowing the Father, we also have the same reason. We are loved, just as Jesus is loved by our Father, as His own sons and daughters.

Second Corinthians 11:3–4 states, "But I fear, lest somehow, as the serpent deceived Eve by his craftiness, so your minds may be corrupted from the simplicity and purity that is in Christ. For if he who comes preaches another Jesus whom we have not preached, or if you receive a different spirit which you have not received, or a different gospel which you have not accepted—you may well put up with it!" The teachings of Jesus Christ and the Gospel of the Good News are simple and pure. We must learn to filter out unwanted doctrines. We must learn what the truth is about the Gospel of peace. We must not be deceived any longer about what Jesus really taught His disciples. We have to stop putting up with the lies that we have accepted as truths.

A good gauge to use when understanding if you are receiving the right teachings concerning the Word of God is if that person, church, or religious establishment is trying to obtain any of God's gifts through works, rather than through righteousness and the grace of God. If so, then they are not correct in their teaching. Another way to tell if the Gospel is being distorted is, ask this question to yourself: Does it build up God's children, or does it tear them down? The true Gospel of Jesus Christ always edifies or builds up; it never tears down or hurts any child of God through judgment or condemnation. Jesus never broke people, He never took from them. He only gave them what they did not have and built them up to the stature that His sacrifice would ultimately elevate them to. First Thessalonians 5:11 says, "Therefore comfort each other and edify one another, just as you also are doing."

Know your Father and know His nature and know what it means to follow the teachings of Jesus our Lord and Savior. Then you will always know the truth of the Gospel. You will not only be at peace, you will also not be able to keep it to yourself. You will have to spread the Good News (the Gospel) to everyone you meet and everyone you know. After all is said and done, isn't that what a disciple of Jesus Christ was instructed to do just before Jesus went to be with our Father? Mark 16:15 commands us, "And He said to them, 'Go into all the world and preach the gospel [Good News] to every creature.'"

13

Question the Status Quo

You have probably come to realize from previous chapters that we as children of God have a problem with the teachings of most religious organizations. Most of this problem lies in the misinterpretation of our Father's nature. Because of the way man has perceived God's nature, they have misunderstood the meaning of His Word. Because of this misunderstanding, there have been countless doctrines adopted by thousands of religious organizations everywhere. The only purpose of this book is that the reader might come to realize the truth about who God really is. And, in turn, may establish a loving relationship with Him.

On my own path to find that relationship, I had to expel many false doctrines from my home church for the sole purpose of moving forward in that relationship.

In order to come to an understanding about some of the fallacies of the teachings of religion, we must first realize that these untruths and inconsistencies exist. Once again, in order to accomplish this, we must go to the Father and His true nature. We must consider what we have learned in previous chapters about the true Word of God and Jesus and His teachings. It is of the utmost importance that we receive the correct teachings or doctrine in order to expel the incorrect teachings that church and religion have so emphatically embraced. This is important to both our relationship with our Father and a joyful and content life here on earth.

Second John 1:9–10 informs us, "Whoever transgresses [goes ahead] and does not abide in the doctrine of Christ does not have God. He who abides in the doctrine of Christ has both the Father and the Son. If anyone comes to you and does not bring this doctrine, do not receive him into your house nor greet him." There has always been someone trying to twist the meaning of what the Father's nature really is, what Jesus did with His finished work, and what the Word of God really means.

It is my hope that you have both read and understood the previous chapters of this book and have begun to see your Father and His nature in a way you have never understood before. And because of this realization, that you have begun to question previous teachings in your life, which have led you to a completely different perspective on both church and your life, than you have ever had before.

You should have begun to understand that your Father is not that judgmental, mean, wrathful God that the majority of His children make Him out to be. You should have begun to understand that everything that has been done with this world was for His children, including creating the world. Your understanding should encompass the fact that our Father is the essence of love itself. That He only wants the very best for His children. And with this particular realization now brought to light, you should understand that He will never judge or punish His children. Ever!

And if you have realized even to a small degree that you may have misjudged your Father and His nature because of the wrong information you received at some point in your life, then you are ready to begin to expel some of the wrong doctrines that have been plaguing your relationship with your Father here on earth.

There have been many times in my life that I have wondered why we do the things we do as a people. I have contemplated the motivation of people, and why exactly do they do what they do. And in the majority of these studies, I have determined one common denominator: The insertion of tradition brought on by what man believed to be the correct way of doing something.

Even in my youth, I noticed that my mother and father brought a certain way of doing things into their relationship. Upon combining their lives into a single cohabitation, they brought with them many new and different traditions, and, in turn, upon combining these traditions, realized many new and different traditions of their own. And I, in turn, have done the same with my wife and children. I am sure that the same is true with the way tradition has and will affect my children and their families.

There is nothing wrong with traditions, either brought from your family as a child or created by a merger of you and your spouse, unless it is a tradition of a church or religious organization. Tradition has no place in your relationship with the Father.

Most of what the church does today is nothing more than a tradition mixed with parts of the Jewish and the Mosaic Law, as well as influences from many pagan religions. These, combined with the misguided teachings of the new converts, corrupted Christianity during the reign of Emperor Constantine. For example, have you ever asked yourself why we dress up to go to worship our Father? It is never said in scripture what kind of garb or attire you are supposed to wear when you go to love and thank your Father. As a matter of fact, the only people that Jesus ever blasted were the religious leaders of His time. He basically said we should not be like them. Not to put on your purple robes (fancy clothes) and parade yourself around so that people think you are more important than you really are.

Luke 20:46 warns us, "Beware of the scribes, who desire to go around in long robes, love greetings in the marketplaces, the best seats in the synagogues, and the best places at feasts." So, in truth, Jesus said *not* to be like what most churches would advocate that you should be.

I would ask you at this point to question two things in every doctrine that you have in your church or religious organization. Why do you do what you do in church? And where did what you do in church or your religious organization come from? I know that what you wear is not a big issue. But by proving the misguided teachings of this one simple point, you may come to question the reason for the thousands of incorrect teachings of the doctrines of religion. These doctrines have been inducted into their teachings, not because it is what should be included, but because of what one person or a group of people deemed best for God's children.

In the case of why some people dress up to go to church, and how it got started the religious leaders and the superspiritual will tell you if you were to ask them the question, they would say, we do so because it is a sign of respect to God. But nowhere in scripture can this statement be proven. The real reason that the churchgoing public dresses up started long before any of our great-grandparents were born. It started even before their grandparents were born. It started with the Roman Emperor Constantine deciding that Rome and all of his empire would become Christians. He claimed that he had a vision from God, and thus, decided that every person within his realm would now be forced into being a Christian. All of this took place about AD 325.

We can surmise from history that the way he and the newly born Catholic Church went about turning pagan nations into God-fearing children, based on violence, torture, and death, was not of the Father's doing. This was one man's attempt of manipulation of God's children, to the obvious outcome of riches and power for both Constantine and the newly born Catholic Church.

The fact that anyone would accept that Constantine was a man of God clearly indicates that they do not know the nature of our Father or the purpose of the finished work of Jesus. If God our Father had intended to use force to convert His children, there would have been no need for the sacrifice of His only begotten Son Jesus Christ. This is a prime example of how the church started down the wrong path of manipulation and tradition. This is nothing more than man's feeble attempt to fix something that God has already corrected, through Jesus.

When Constantine made all of these provinces of his kingdom comply with the incorrect teaching of Christianity, he stated that they must do away with their pagan religions and embrace a new Christian religion. The main problem with this is the fact that his empire was so vast that he could not ensure that every person in his realm was complying with the new teachings. And as politics would have it, he appointed men from the church to go to these districts and make sure that they were doing what they were supposed to do. And because most inspectors of anything are predictable, these inspections would stay on a very predictable schedule. Whenever the inspectors were scheduled to inspect a certain district, the region in question would quit their worship of pagan idols and demigods, dress up, and act like Christians because of the fear of punishment.

Many of our traditions of worship have been carried through the centuries because of this particular place in time. The clergy, upon realizing that they could not stop the way that these pagans worship, decided to make a compromise of what they would tolerate. And because of this, many things in our church today have no basis in scripture. We must realize that with the finished work of Jesus Christ, God never uses manipulation or fear to bring His children back to him. Love and forgiveness are the only motivating factors in the relationship with your Father.

We need to understand what the difference between repentance and penance is. "Repentance" is the changing of your mind, through all that God has provided for you through the finished work of Jesus Christ. "Penance" is a misconception provided to us by the Catholic Church that states when you become cognizant of your sin, you must punish yourself to a degree worthy of the sin. Penance has no place in the new covenant. Penance is nothing more than works righteousness, or trying to establish your own righteousness through something you do, or don't do.

The people that Constantine tried to convert to Christianity converted because of something they were trying to do and not because of a changed mind. This tradition is carried on in the church today. Nowhere in Jesus' teachings does it tell us that as Christians, we are to go into the entire world and force people into submission to God and their salvation. On the contrary, Jesus teaches us to show the world, through love, who the Father is, and what salvation really means. But because of the thinking of the Roman government at the time that the Catholic Church was established, we as Christians feel compelled to show that our God is bigger than their God.

The Romans were a conquering people, a warring people. And therefore they had a mentality that stated, if we can conquer your country and your people, this must mean that we have conquered your God also. So, in essence, what they were saying is, if our empire is bigger than yours, then our God must be bigger than yours. This is just one more fallacy that was born out of the era of Roman conquest.

The Jewish people could not get the fact that Jesus did not come as a conqueror because they were taught that the Messiah would come as a conqueror when He came. This teaching has infiltrated the church of today. Jesus came as a Savior not a conqueror. Never judge your Father's power by the stupidity of the world's standard. What was done by Constantine and the Catholic Church was not done for the betterment of God's kingdom. It was done for the betterment of man's power and greed.

Upon closer examination, we discover a few facts that shed some light on the dark history of Rome and the Vatican. In the name of God, Vatican City took over every trade of every country in the world that they came in contact with, enslaving God's children to do their bidding, not for the betterment of mankind, but so that the church might gain wealth and power. This would include but not be limited to the trade of silk in the Orient and coffee and tea in many other countries.

Do not take my word for it. If you have questions about what I am writing, look deeper into the history of the Catholic Church. You will not find the nature of our Father there. But what you will find are many traditions borne out of the Catholic religion that are inherently wrong. If you wish to have a local proof of this, go on the mission tour in San Antonio, Texas, and you will find on a small scale what the Catholic Church has been doing since its birth. They admittedly took the natives of that region and forced them into a life of bondage to grow food and work, not for themselves or their benefit, but for the church, so that the Catholic Church's wealth and power might be increased.

Vatican City is the smallest country in the world, and it is also the richest country in the world. They have no form of export or import from or to any country. The only commodity that they can lay claim to is religion.

I fear that this weakness for power and wealth has carried over from the Catholic Church. Many of our churches today are Christian not for the furtherance of the Gospel or the spreading of the Good News of Christ and the salvation that He brought. Instead, they are playing church with their own agenda for power and wealth.

The reason I have gone so deep down this rabbit hole is to make you realize that every church can be traced back to the Lutheran Church, and the Lutheran Church stems directly off the Catholic Church. And the Catholic Church is dead wrong in understanding the nature of our Father. Therefore, a lot of the traditions of the modern church are just as wrong and misguided as the church that gave birth to them.

If you would truly examine the history of your church and its origin, you will find this to be true. And if you will study how the Catholic Church and the Jewish synagogue function, you will find many remarkable similarities.

Why do Christians have an altar in their churches? The word used for "altar" in the *Strong's Exhaustive Concordance* before Jesus came to earth is #4196, and this word is never used again in the same context in the New Testament. Its meaning is completely changed with the finished work of Jesus. The meaning of the word #4196 means to slay an animal or sacrifice. But after Jesus arrives on earth, the word #2379 means a view or a sight. There is no reason any longer to have an altar.

When "altar" is mentioned in the New Testament, it is only to say that we no longer have need of it. This tradition was nothing more than a carryover from the Jewish teaching before the finished work of Jesus Christ.

You might ask yourself at this point, is it wrong to have an altar? Yes, because if any time you feel that you need to go somewhere special to get in touch with your Father, you will not realize that you carried that relationship with you 24 hours a day, seven days a week.

Because of some of the misguided teachings such as the altar and that the church is a building that you go into for worship, we are inhibited in attaining that true and wonderful relationship with our Father. Anything in religion that would cause this breach in your relationship with Him is wrong.

This is one of the main points that the writers of the New Testament were trying to prevent from happening. When the apostle Paul was writing letters to

Timothy, he was trying to explain anything and everything that he could think of that would help this young man lead his church. He tried to tell Timothy how to solve the problems that he was going to encounter with the people of that church. And when we examine the contents of First and Second Timothy, we find that most of the problems revolve around letting the wrong teachings into the church.

First Timothy 4:1–2 says, "Now the Spirit expressly [explicitly] says that in latter times some will depart from the faith, giving heed to deceiving spirits and doctrines of demons, speaking lies in hypocrisy, having their own conscience seared with a hot iron." Second Timothy 4:3–4 says, "For the time will come when they will not endure sound doctrine, but according to their own desires, because they have itching ears, they will heap up for themselves teachers; and they will turn their ears away from the truth, and be turned aside to fables."

Paul was explaining that the Spirit that is guiding him is clear on this matter about what is going to happen in the latter times (last days). There is a lot of talk about us being in the last days. We are now in the last days. We have been in the last days since Jesus completed His work. The problems in the church today are no different than the problems of the first-century church. And if this is the case, then we should be able to find something in God's Word to help with this particular problem. We must use the Word of God to see what is the correct teaching or doctrine. We must filter everything through God's Spirit in us, through the knowledge of the nature of our Father, through the finished work of our Lord Jesus, and a realization that everything has been accomplished for us in the world.

We must first understand and accept that there is a problem. Because if we do not acknowledge that there is a problem, we will never make an attempt to correct it.

We cannot assume that the problems of the first-century church were corrected after these letters were written. If we accept the fact that the church today is no better at receiving the gifts of our Father or the fact that we are a new man because of the finished work of Jesus than the churches that Paul is writing to, then and only then can the necessary correction be made. All of these churches that Paul addressed were trying to add something to what was already completed by God through Jesus.

Colossians 2:20–23 states, "Therefore, if you died with Christ from the basic principles of the world, why, as though living in the world, do you subject yourselves to regulations—'Do not touch, do not taste, do not handle,' which all concern things which perish with the using—according to the commandments and doctrines of men? These things indeed have an appearance of wisdom in self-imposed religion, false humility, and neglect of the body, but are of no value against the indulgence of the flesh."

We must always examine church doctrine through the nature of our Father and His Word. Always question the reason why you are to do something, the way you are doing it, and demand proof, or prove it to yourself. If when you start to ask questions about religion you get a response of negativity, remember there is nothing hidden from you by God because you are His beloved child. If the truth about the doctrine that you are being taught is obscure, then you must realize that it was made that way by man, not by your Father. Know in your heart that you are a son or daughter of the only God. Do not be deceived about who your Father is. Do not be misled about what He has always wanted for you as His child. And as God's child, you are in charge. Your Father and Jesus gave you this commission. The only thing that can prevent you from doing and being what you were meant to do and be is an inability to separate the truth from the lies.

Ephesians 4:13–14 states, "till we all come to the unity of the faith and of the knowledge of the Son of God, to a perfect man, to the measure of the stature of the fullness of Christ; that we should no longer be children, tossed to and fro and carried about with every wind of doctrine, by the trickery of men, in the cunning craftiness of deceitful plotting."

In order for God's church to shine above everything else in the world, we must agree on the truth of God's Word. And the only way that this can be done is by the elimination of man-made doctrine, so that the true doctrine of Christ might be seen and understood by not only His children, but also seen by the rest of the world.

Ephesians 4:17–18 says, "This I say, therefore, and testify in the Lord, that you should no longer walk as the rest of the Gentiles walk, in the futility of their mind, having their understanding darkened, being alienated from the life of God, because of the ignorance that is in them, because of the blindness of their heart." Open your heart to the truth and be ready to light up your understanding and live the life of a child of God that you were always intended to live.

The scriptures that I have quoted in this book are a drop of water in the ocean compared to the proof that exists in God's Word. But due to the lack of space, because I would have to copy almost the entire New Testament, I could not show you everything you need to know in debunking all the misguided traditions that need correcting. It is my sincere hope that you would research deeper into God's Word and its meaning, and, in turn, come to realize the only truth that there is. The rest is up to you, whether you sit back and trust the teachings that you are receiving or choose to question the status quo.

14

Ifs, Ands, or Buts

When trying to understand and interpret the Word of God it is imperative that you understand two things. You must understand how to discern the whole meaning of the verse and not just a line or two, even if this means you need to go all the way back to the beginning of what the writer is writing about. Sometimes this will even entail looking up the meaning of the word in the original language. This does not mean, however, that you need to go back to school and learn Hebrew, Greek, and Aramaic. There are books available and information on the Internet that will provide more than adequate answers to all of your questions about what a particular word or phrase means. You must first have the desire to search for the truth, and then you will always find it.

Even more important than the research of the contents of the Bible is the understanding of one simple word. The word I am referring to is the word "but." Because of a misunderstanding of this three-letter word, millions of God's children leave church every Sunday beguiled and confused by the teachers who have misrepresented who God's children really are because they failed to finish a judgmental sermon or teaching with the word "but," in it, followed by an explanation of how, and because of this word, everything I said previously is now null and void because of the word "but."

In order to understand how important the word "but" is, we must first agree on its meaning. Let's say for the sake of understanding that you had a person call you on the phone. You know, the one that always calls just as you and your family are about to sit down and enjoy a good meal or watch a good movie. You pick up the phone, a little agitated with the timing of the caller. After you say hello, the person on the other end immediately begins to tell you about your good fortune. They go on to explain that you are the winner of everything that you have always dreamed of in your entire life. They do not stop explaining until they have told you that everything is free.

You, being wise to this particular form of coercion, are waiting for that one single word. What is that word? The word is "but." Any time that word is placed in a written form or in a conversation, it means that the statement made just prior to the word "but" has now changed. And this statement just after the word "but" will explain the change in the statement just prior to the word "but." This is usually done by the words "if" or "and," followed by the criteria of the explanation.

For example; if you will read this entire book I want to give each of you a new car of your choice, *but!* I do not have the means to do this, so I am not going to give you a new car. The point is that I am not Elvis or Oprah, and I am not going to give you a new car. And the one word that changes the statement concerning the fact that I am not going to give you a new car is the word "but."

The Bible is filled with the word "but." In the New Testament between Romans and Revelations the word "but" is used 186 times. You would think that the church would start teaching about the importance of this word in your first class at Sunday school as a child. But they do not!

In search of more proof, let us go to Mr. Webster's definition rather than my own. This definition states, "but, accept, otherwise, other than, on the contrary, or with the exception of." Now it is official. The word "but" changes the meaning of everything said before it.

Have you ever heard a teaching in church about how you are a sinner, and if you say that you are not a sinner you are a liar and the truth is not in you? The misinterpretation of this concept is found in 1 John 1:6–9 which says, "If we say that we have fellowship with Him, and walk in darkness, we lie and do not practice the truth. But if we walk in the light as He is in the light, we have a fellowship with one another, and the blood of Jesus Christ His Son cleanses us from all sin. If we say that we have no sin, we deceive ourselves, and the truth is not in us. If we confess our sins, He is faithful and just to forgive us our sins and to cleanse us from all unrighteousness."

It is important that we take a look at another word that is almost always with the word "but." It is the word "if." The word "if," when placed next to or just after the word "but," gives the reason why there is a change in the previous statement. Even when the word "but" is not present, you can almost always add the word "but" next to the word "if" to understand the change in the previous statement.

For example, in the above verse, John is telling us that if we walk in the darkness (or away from the truth) we are lying (to ourselves). But if (something has changed in the above statement) we walk in the light we now have fellowship with God. The change in this verse was made after the words "but" and "if." Now it says that you do practice the truth if you do a certain action (walk in the light).

The verse goes on to say that it is because of our fellowship with Christ that we are able to walk in the light. Then the word "if" is used again to change the verse and gives reason for the change. The last "if" (but if) found in these verses explain that every change that has been made to the original statement is now understood. The verse tells you something about what you were before you became what you are now. You were walking in darkness because of your denial of the truth about your problem.

A problem will never be solved if you do not recognize it as a problem. But if we recognize the problem, then we will work toward a solution. We will change our minds (repent). If there is no changing of your mind (no repentance), then we are lying to ourselves, or we are in denial (deny the truth). But if we confess (or admit) our problem is sin, then God our Father is faithful to forgive us and make us righteous.

Remember, being righteous is the requirement to enter into heaven and be with our Father. Everything prior to the last part of this statement does not apply to you if you are, in fact, a child of God. We must stop trying to make verses apply to our lives that have no validity in our lives. According to this, all that you need to do is walk in the light, because now with that righteousness from God, you will practice the truth.

Notice how it says "practice the truth." When you practice something it is because you have not mastered it. Realize that you will never master the Word of God. But if our righteousness depends on confession of sins and practicing the truth, then we are righteous. And with this realization, when you fall down, and you *will* fall down, you will see this for what it is: you just fell down. Never take the fact that you have fallen as a sign that your relationship with your Father has changed in any way. Just get up, dust yourself off, and keep practicing the truth.

The one thing you must never do is give up on the Father. He will never give up on you. He will not even change His mind about who you are, His beloved child. From the time that you establish a relationship with Him until the end of everything as we know it, He will claim you as His own.

I hope that you are beginning to understand the importance of these words in the overall meaning of God's Word. Let us take a look at a few more verses, so that you can get the hang of this. And then you can get your Bible and see God's Word in a whole new perspective.

First Corinthians 15:56–57 tells us, "The sting of death is sin, and the strength of sin is the law. But thanks be to God, who gives us the victory through our Lord Jesus Christ." Everyone throughout time has feared death, and religion has held both sin and death over the heads of God's children since its inception. Look for the word "but" in these verses and understand that the strength that death and sin had was taken away by Jesus for us.

We are taught that the opposite of love would be hate. But it is not. The opposite of love is fear. 1 John 4:18 says, "There is no fear in love; but perfect love casts out fear, because fear involves torment. But he who fears has not been made perfect in love."

If you will read all of chapter 4 you will discover the reason for the word "but." You have been made perfect in love through Jesus and the Spirit of God. And because of this fact, you should never fear anything or anyone; this includes your Father.

Always look for the words "but" and "if." You will come to realize that there is a misinterpretation of most of scripture because of a failure to recognize these words. And because of this misinterpretation there is a failure to recognize who we are, as God's children.

When we read anything in scripture or any other book, we relate to one of the characters in the story.

Our problem is when we read the Bible we put ourselves in the place where the church has taught us that we belong. In order to realize who you are, you must first begin to put yourself in the proper perspective in scripture. Let us say, for instance, that you are reading about Jesus and how He went from town to town healing the sick with His apostles. In this story you have an option of many characters with which to relate. You will ultimately relate to one or more characters in every story that you read. In this story, you have the options of relating to the onlooker, the sick person needing to be healed, a disciple, or Jesus the Son of God.

Most people, because of their teaching, will choose the person of the lowest standing when relating to a story in the Bible because we have failed to accept the truth of who we are now. We still see ourselves as who we were before we were saved from sin. It is because of these wrong teachings that we never perceived our place when trying to understand the teachings of our Lord Jesus. The Bible and its teachings are the only place that we do this. If we were reading a book or watching a movie, you would never relate to the victim or the villain. We almost always relate to the hero or the heroine of the book or movie. But religion teaches us never to put ourselves in the place of Jesus, which would be blasphemy—when, in fact, everything that Jesus teaches His disciples revolve around how to act just like Him, in every way, shape, and form.

We are told that we are His disciples and that we should mirror His every move, style, and action. We are told to mimic everything that Jesus said and did, the way He said and did these things. We are to be His followers, or disciples, in every way possible.

But because of religion, we are taught never to put ourselves in His place when reading about His life and teachings. This is a direct contradiction of religion and discipleship. If, when you read about Jesus, you do not put yourself in that role that He is in, then you will never see yourself as God's child or Jesus' friend and brother.

First John 4:17 explains, "Love has been perfected among us in this: that we may have boldness in the day of judgment; because as He is, so are we in this world." It is imperative when we read God's Word that we put ourselves in the role that you were destined to be in, the role of the Son of God. Jesus our Lord and Savior left us in charge of the world when He went to sit at the right hand of our Father. But because we failed to recognize this fact, we never will be able to take charge of this world. Never be afraid to be what God made you through Jesus' finished work.

Look at the "ifs," "ands," and "buts" from the perspective of a son or daughter of God and you will begin to see not only your new nature, but also the unchanging nature of your Father. Always read God's Word with a view of love and forgiveness, always knowing that everything that is written is for your benefit, and that you are a beloved child of God. Religious people will tell you that this is wrong teaching, but I say judge for yourself by your spirit and the Word of God.

First Corinthians 2:12–16 says, "Now we have received, not the spirit of the world, but the Spirit who is from God, that we might know the things that have been freely given to us by God. These things we also speak, not in words which man's wisdom teaches but which the Holy Spirit teaches, comparing spiritual things with spiritual. But the natural man does not receive the things of the Spirit of God, for they are foolishness to him; nor can he know them, because they are spiritually discerned. But he who is spiritual judges all things, yet he himself is rightly judged by no one. For 'who has known the mind of the Lord that he may instruct Him?' But we have the mind of Christ."

This plainly tells us many things about anyone who would say to you that it is wrong to feel like you are a son or a daughter of God. It says you should not look at things the way the world sees them. It says to be wise you need to have the perception of God's Spirit in you. It says that everyone who does not see with the Spirit, but sees with the view of the world, will think that you and everyone like you are foolish. It also says that you are right in your thinking, and no man has the right to judge you. The reason we are who we are is explained in the word "but." "*But* we have the mind of Christ."

If, when you are reading God's Word, you feel like the meaning you are receiving is against the nature of your loving Father, simply look for the words "if," "and," or "but." You will find that it was misread, misquoted, or misunderstood, because your Father's loving and forgiving nature has never change. And even more important than this is the fact that His loving and forgiving nature will never change.

15
Grace, Not Your Ability

Grace is probably one of the most misunderstood gifts that our Father has provided for His children. If you were to ask most of the churchgoing public to explain what the definition of God's grace means to them, most of them, if not all, will tell you grace is no more than God's wonderful forgiveness for His children. They make statements similar to "I am a sinner saved by grace." This is an incorrect and extremely damaging statement. If God's children truly understood the intricate workings of salvation and all that it provides, then this same statement would sound something like this: "I was a sinner, but now I am saved from that sin because of God's divine influence upon my heart and my life. Because of His grace (divine influence), there is a reflection of that influence in my life."

If you look into the Greek definition, these are the exact words used in the *Strong's Exhaustive Concordance of the Bible* for the Greek word *charis* means exactly that. "Grace" is God's own influence in your heart, or at the center of your life, that will enable you to do the things you could never hope to accomplish on your own.

Once again, our Father has provided us with exactly the right gift needed to overcome sin and live a wonderful, blessed, and joyful life. However, the teachings of wrong doctrines will not accept the truth that God has provided everything needed for salvation and that abundant life. We, as His children, are not required to do anything but believe and confess our need for these gifts provided by our Father.

The statement that I made earlier in the paragraph proves their inability to accept the fact of grace saving you from sin. You are not a sinner saved by grace. You are either a sinner, or you are a saved individual. You cannot be saved and a sinner at the same time. It is similar to falling into the water and not being able to swim. Due to your own lack of ability to swim, you would have surely drowned. But upon seeing your plight, someone throws you a life preserver. After taking a firm hold of the life preserver, you are then pulled from the water onto the land, and are now in no danger of drowning.

It would sound ludicrous for you to say, I am a drowning man or woman saved by the life preserver. You have either drowned, or you were saved. You cannot do both. It is one way or the other. If you say you are saved by God's divine influence (Grace), then you are saved. This means you can no longer say that you are a sinner, because when you make a confession that you are still a sinner, you are making a statement that God's divine influence and its reflection in your life is inadequate to change the fact that you were a sinner. You are, in essence, saying, that the finished work of our Lord Jesus Christ was insufficient to accomplish what it was intended to accomplish.

First Timothy 1:13–14 states, "although I was formerly a blasphemer, a persecutor, and an insolent man; but I obtained mercy because I did it ignorantly in unbelief. And the grace of our Lord was exceedingly abundant, with faith and love which are in Christ Jesus." Second Corinthians 12:9 says, "And He said to me, 'My grace is sufficient for you, for My strength is made perfect in weakness.'" The bigger sinner you were, the more abundant God's grace will appear in your life. The weaker the person you were, the stronger the person you will become, because through grace (God's ability), you are made strong.

Grace, like all of the gifts from our Father, is contingent on the acceptance of that gift. Ephesians 3:6–7 informs us, "that the Gentiles should be fellow heirs, of the same body, and partakers of His promise in Christ through the gospel, of which I became a minister according to the gift of the grace of God given to me by the effective working of His power."

Almost every letter written to the first-century churches started with the writer telling the recipients that they were praying they would receive grace. First Corinthians 1:3 says, "Grace to you and peace from God our Father and the Lord Jesus Christ." And in almost every instance these letters ended with the same thought. First Corinthians 16:23 says, "The grace of our Lord Jesus Christ be with you." The writers of these letters knew how important it was to know and understand that it was the gift of God's divine influence that would determine the change in their lives. The reliance on our own ability is a simple act of futility when it comes to salvation. There is absolutely nothing that we can do on our own to perpetuate this change of sin and procure salvation in our life.

Many people, after being saved, fail to understand the intricate workings of salvation and the process that Grace is destined to take in their lives. They have a misconception of exactly how salvation works. They are led to believe that because they have understood that they were a sinner, and therefore confessed that fact and now have accepted Jesus as their personal Savior, that everything will work out fine. They understood that they were washed, with not only the baptism of water, but also the baptism of the Holy Spirit, and that now they are a new person. They also understand that because of Jesus, they are free from sin in their lives. What they do not understand is why the world did not mysteriously change into that wonderful blessed world that everyone was talking about just before they got saved.

To put it simply, they wonder why their life is no different than it was before they were saved, why is it so hard to say, "I am not a sinner"? The main reason is that no one tells them this is the beginning of the change to becoming a new person, the new person that is talked about in scripture. They do not explain to that newly saved individual about all the wonderful gifts from their Father that are now available to them. They do not teach that these gifts are imperative for the transition to become that new person. To escape from a worldly life to a godly life is not in their ability but in God's ability and the gifts that He has provided for them.

Because of their lack of understanding, religion fails to explain to the new believer that if these gifts remained unopened, he or she will never make the transition from the cross to a life of peace and joy. They fail to explain to a new believer that along with the gift of salvation, the gifts of righteousness, peace, joy, the adoption into the family of God, and grace (God's ability in your heart to make that change in your life) are also included.

Instead, the religious community tries to convince a new believer that they need to try hard to change all the bad in their lives now that they are saved individuals. However, no one can change into someone just because religion has determined that you should be different. Ephesians 2:4–9 says, "But God, who is rich in mercy, because of His great love with which He loved us, even when we were dead in trespasses, made us alive together with Christ (by grace you have been saved), and raised us up together, and made us sit together in the heavenly places in Christ Jesus, that in the ages to come He might show the exceeding riches of His grace in His kindness toward us in Christ Jesus. For by grace you have been saved through faith, and that not of yourselves; it is the gift of God, not of works, lest anyone should boast."

With a religious mind-set, you will always fall short of your expectations in your own mind. And with the inadequacy of your own ability, you will always consider yourself to be a sinner. You will always doubt not only that the Father loves you, but also you will eventually come to doubt your own salvation from moment to moment and sin to sin. It is imperative that you change this way of thinking. You must relinquish all of the responsibility of the change in your life to the workings of grace (God's ability).

First Peter 1:13 exhorts us, "Therefore gird up the loins of your mind, be sober, and rest your hope fully upon the grace that is to be brought to you at the revelation of Jesus Christ." It is through the knowledge of what Jesus did with His death, burial, and resurrection that the gifts of our Father work in our lives.

If you believe in Jesus and His teachings, then you are a saved disciple of His. Guard your mind against all other teachings. Put all of your hope, not in your own limited understanding and abilities, but instead, rely on God your Father and His grace, and His ability to work in your heart and make the necessary changes in your life. If you have not denied your Lord Jesus Christ, then you have not lost God's ability (grace) to work in you, to accomplish everything that He intended to accomplish from the beginning of salvation. Anyone who tells you they quit sinning the moment they were saved is a liar. That is simply not the way the process works.

You will definitely change into a new person if you will allow God's grace and all of His gifts to work in you. However, this change can only take place with the acceptance of the gifts provided by your Father. It will take time and understanding of how these gifts work in your life to complete the process. Time and understanding have nothing to do with your salvation, just your transition.

To put it as simply as I can, if you are saved from death and sin by the finished work of our Lord Jesus Christ, then you are saved from death and sin. Look at sin in this way. Everyone has the ability to lie and steal. But just because you have the ability to lie and steal, that does not mean that you are a liar and a thief. In the same way, everyone has the ability to sin, but just having this ability does not make you a sinner. This works in the same way as righteousness.

Righteousness can only come from God. But because Jesus has finished His work, we now have the righteousness of God. So then, grace, or God's ability to overcome sin, also abides in us. Jesus had the same ability that we are given to overcome temptation through grace. Temptation is not sin! Only after you succumb to temptation does it become sin. Scripture plainly tells us that Jesus was tempted by sin, but because He used all of the gifts of His Father to their full potential, including grace, or God's influence on His heart, He was able to stop sin at temptation. Therefore, Jesus never sinned.

You have access to that same God-given ability in your life. You have had access to that ability since the moment you were saved. But because of the lack of understanding of the gift of grace, we, as God's children, do not utilize the gift of grace when confronted with temptation. If we would only recognize and use this wonderful gift, sin would no longer be an issue in our lives.

Religion has so misconstrued the meaning of God's gifts. We are taught that we should be able to fight the good fight on our own. As I have said many times in this book, you alone have nothing to do with your salvation and happiness, other than to believe and accept the gifts of your loving Father and let them do the work in your life.

The main problem in utilizing the gifts that God has provided for every one of His children is not that they refuse to use the gifts; it is that they refuse to believe that God's gifts exist. Or they refuse to believe that the gifts are for them because they think of themselves as unworthy to receive anything so wonderful from God Himself. Once again, it is because of the unbelief that they stay in bondage.

It is always about the choices that you make both before and after you are saved that determines what kind of life we will live. If you continue to make choices based on the person that you were before you were saved, then the outcome of these choices will be the same as they were before you were saved. In order for your life to change, you must open and utilize the gifts of your Father. This simply means, you must stop looking at the world around you in the same way as you did before you became a child of God. Stop doing the same thing over and over, expecting a different result. This is, in essence, the definition of insanity.

Act like the man or woman that you are now, not the person you were before. Never make a decision again without filtering that decision through the gifts and knowledge at your disposal provided by your Father.

Try to think of it this way. You are driving your car on a long trip. As you drive along you notice a noise coming from the front right side of your car. After pulling your car to the shoulder and inspecting the location of the noise, you realize that you now have a flat tire. This is a very bad discovery for two reasons. You are 70 miles from the nearest civilization. And you just remember that there was a question about the spare tire when you bought the car just a few days ago. You seem to remember that there was not a spare in the trunk on the day that you purchased the car. So instead of inspecting the trunk to see if there is a spare tire, because you are certain there is not, you start walking toward what you hope will be your rescue out of this situation, never knowing that the dealer where you bought the car found your spare tire and had a man place it in the trunk while you were signing the annoying paperwork for the purchase of that car. In all of the confusion, the salesman forgot to tell you this fact.

Yes, you have a more-than-adequate spare tire, conveniently hidden, underneath the mat in the trunk of your car. But because you believe that there is no spare tire in your new car, you have made the choice to handle this situation in the most difficult way possible. This is exactly the same as having God's gifts at our disposal and not using them because we do not believe we have them. If you do not believe God's gifts are there for you to use, then you will never look for them, and you will never use them.

It is not about what you can do on your own, it is about how well you have learned to utilize the gifts of God's ability to work in your life. These gifts are just that; they are gifts. They are free; they cost you nothing. They are yours to have and to use at your discretion. God will never take any of these gifts from you based on your performance. God is not that kind of Father. It is not God's nature to lie, and He said that He would never be mad at us again. His gifts are intended for you to use to overcome any and all shortcomings that exist in this world and our lives.

Romans 12:2 exhorts us, "And do not be conformed to this world, but be transformed by the renewing of your mind, that you may prove what is that good and acceptable and perfect will of God." You need to change your mind (repent) from the wisdom of the world. Allow God's grace (God's divine influence on your heart) to transform you. Then, and only then, will you be that joyful child, free from the pain of sin, in this world.

Prove to yourself what the perfect will of God really is, which every one of His children should come to realize. If God's children would only understand what He has done through the finished work of Jesus Christ. Then not one of His children would be lost or unhappy, and every one of His children would seek and find a loving, peaceful relationship with Him. And they would know "what is that good and acceptable and perfect will of God" and what has always been.

16
Flex Your Faith Muscle

As it is that most of the gifts from our Father, faith is no exception. Religion has so distorted what faith really is that God's children have become ineffective in the use of faith. They have reduced faith to a basic definition, limited by their own inadequate understanding. And because they have failed to realize what faith is, they have stayed in the dark to the possibilities of its infinite potential accomplishments.

In order to change the way that you perceive faith and the way that faith should work in your life, we will again go to the definition in *Strong's Exhaustive Concordance of the Bible.* We find the Greek definition of the word "faith" is represented by the number 4102. This word is found 239 times in the New Testament. It is found every time the word "faith" is used except for four times when it refers to a small or little faith. It means to believe or to be faithful, but it really means so much more than that.

Upon closer examination of the word, you'll find that it comes from the root word number 3982 which means "agree as sure, believe, have confidence, make friends, obeyed, persuade, trust, or yield." Every one of these definitions of the word "faith" would imply that there is something that we have to do to get faith to work correctly.

Hopefully, you will read this chapter with the mind-set of an instruction manual for faith. And not only see faith for what it is, but also use faith the way that Jesus used faith, the way that God intended that we should use faith. Faith, as with all other gifts from our Father, will make a drastic change in your life. And not only in your life, but in the lives that surround you, including the rest of the world.

The first stop in our understanding on the journey to using the gift of faith is the realization of where it comes from. Faith comes straight from your Father Himself. God is a just and loving God, and it is not in His nature to give you a gift and not give you the instruction book on how to use that gift. However, as with all of the gifts from your Father, you need to know your Father and His intentions for the gift to work correctly. Hebrews 11:6 states, "But without faith it is impossible to please Him, for he who comes to God must believe that He is, and that He is a rewarder of those who diligently seek Him."

Without faith you cannot please God because you will not believe that God exists. But if you believe that God exists, and that He is your Father, and that He supplied everything needed for salvation and an abundant life through the finished work of our Lord Jesus Christ, then you have fulfilled the requirements of the above verse and need to move on to the next part of this verse. This part states that when you have sought out a relationship with your Father, He wants to reward you when you find Him.

Galatians 5:6 says, "For in Christ Jesus neither circumcision nor uncircumcision avails anything, but faith working through love." We are to understand through this verse that since we have fulfilled these requirements, that we please God very much, and therefore, we have the faith we need to accomplish everything that this gift provides for us and the rest of the world.

How much faith do you have? The answer to this question is simply: enough. Everyone was given the same amount of faith. Romans 12:3 states, "For I say, through the grace given to me, to everyone who is among you, not to think of himself more highly than he ought to think, but to think soberly, as God has dealt to each one a measure of faith."

According to this verse, you have a measure of faith, the same measure as everyone else. If you have the same measure of faith as everyone else, why do some people have great faith and others have small faith? When you were born, you were born with all of the muscles that you have now. You did not gain or lose any muscles as you grew and got older and stronger. In fact, you have the same muscles as Mr. Universe. The difference is, your muscles are not as developed as the muscles of the man that holds the Mr. Universe title.

Your faith muscle works in much the same way as your body muscle does. When you were born-again, faith began to work in your life. Galatians 3:22–26 states, "But the Scripture has confined all under sin, that the promise by faith in Jesus Christ might be given to those who believe. But before faith came, we were kept under guard by the law, kept for the faith which would afterward be revealed. Therefore the law was our tutor to bring us to Christ, that we might be justified by faith. But after faith has come, we are no longer under a tutor. For you are all sons of God through faith in Christ Jesus."

Just like the muscles of a newborn baby, you have everything you need, but the muscles must be developed. Your faith muscle must also be developed, or made stronger. Just like a newborn baby who cannot walk or even hold its own head up, your faith muscle is just as weak and in need of exercise when you have been reborn into God's family. And just like the muscles in your body, what you're able to accomplish will depend on how much exercise you give that muscle. The more you work your faith muscle, the stronger it gets; the stronger it gets, the more you will be able to accomplish with faith. The more you are able to accomplish with your faith muscle, the better your life and the lives of those around you will become.

Everyone has the same faith, but not everyone's faith is developed to the same strength. Jesus tells us that the amount of faith needed to do great things is miniscule. Matthew 17:20 clearly tells us, "So Jesus said to them, 'Because of your unbelief; for assuredly, I say to you, if you have faith as a mustard seed, you will say to this mountain, "Move from here to there," and it will move; and nothing will be impossible for you.'"

Even if we are given the smallest measure of faith that you can think of, Jesus tells us that this is enough faith to do anything. The reason why God's children are not moving mountains or accomplishing the impossible must be in the development of our faith muscle and the way that we use that faith muscle.

How do we exercise our faith muscle so that we, as God's children, can do all the great and wonderful things that are promised in our Father's Word? By having a personal relationship with your Father and by understanding His nature. And also by knowing your Lord and Savior Jesus Christ and what He accomplished. Then you and I could have this ability. The only way to get to know God your Father and your brother Jesus is by spending time to get to know them. You must establish a relationship with them.

The only true way to know the Father is by His Word and the example that was set for us by Jesus, His only begotten Son. This should not be a hard task. After all, Jesus already lives in your heart. Consider Ephesians 3:17: "that Christ may dwell in your hearts through faith; that you, being rooted and grounded in love…" Notice that Jesus lives in you because of faith and that this faith is yours because of love not fear.

Your relationship with your Father can only be established through the knowledge of His loving nature. It is through the understanding of who your Father is and what He has done through Jesus that a lasting relationship will develop between you and your Father. And with this understanding of God's nature and your place in His plan your faith muscle will continue to grow stronger.

The best way to see the potential of any tool is to use it for hard work. And if you want to see how strong you are or what you can lift, just try to pick up something. The problem with God's children is they have been convinced that they are too weak to try anything. And when they do try, they quit without understanding that they just need to get a little stronger. They need to exert the effort to exercise their faith muscle until they can succeed at their endeavor.

The more you know about your Father's nature, the stronger your faith will become. And the only way to know His nature is to spend time learning about Him and spending time with Him, apart from the world. This will always establish a lasting relationship with your Father.

You must understand that church is a building not a relationship with God. Romans 10:8–9 informs us, "But what does it say? 'The word is near you, in your mouth and in your heart' (that is, the word of faith which we preach): that if you confess with your mouth the Lord Jesus and believe in your heart that God has raised Him from the dead, you will be saved."

Romans 10:17 states, "So then faith comes by hearing, and hearing by the word of God." For faith to grow stronger, you must understand what the true Gospel is, what faith is, and what God's love has done for you. Your faith muscle can only get stronger with exercise, and it can only get exercise by hearing and believing the true Word of God. Always filter who you are and what you can accomplish through your Father's loving nature. Never filter your belief through what man and his doctrines have misconstrued as to who God is and what He wants for His children.

First Corinthians 2:4–5 says, "And my speech and my preaching were not with persuasive words of human wisdom, but in demonstration of the Spirit and of power, that your faith should not be in the wisdom of men but in the power of God."

If you will learn to exercise your faith muscle in the power and wisdom of God your Father, it will continue to grow stronger. But if you exercise your faith muscle in man's wisdom and its lack of power, you will stay as you have always been—as weak as a newborn baby.

Know without a doubt who you are. Have confidence of your status as an adopted child, belonging to the one and only God. Write this on your heart: "My Father is always for me; He is never against me; He has already given me everything I need in this world, and everything I need in my relationship with Him. I never have to beg my Father for anything. I'm never alone or forsaken. I am not trying to convince my Father to do something that He does not want to do. He has already done everything for me that could possibly be done for my benefit, not because I am worthy, but because of His great love." If you can understand these statements and turn them into belief, your faith muscle will grow exponentially. You will accomplish everything that God's Word says you can accomplish.

Philemon 6 says, "that the sharing of your faith may become effective by the acknowledgment of every good thing which is in you in Christ Jesus." Realize that you have the gifts and the ability to become effective and show God's power in the world. Write it on your heart that faith is a gift, given to us along with all of the other gifts. It's free of cost to us since it has already been paid for by Jesus.

The only thing that we are required to do is accept and learn how to use these gifts. But it is not about what you can do, it is about what you accept. Can you accept all that has been done for you? Hebrews 12:1–2 states, "Therefore we also, since we are surrounded by so great a cloud of witnesses, let us lay aside every weight, and the sin which so easily ensnares us, and let us run with endurance the race set before us, looking unto Jesus, the author and finisher of our faith, who for the joy that was set before Him endured the cross, despising the shame, and has sat down at the right hand of the throne of God."

These verses plainly tell us to get rid of any and all weights or problems of this world, and this includes sin consciousness. That our work (spreading the Gospel) that we were given would be accomplished by remembering that Jesus is the organizer and the perfecter of our faith. That He has finished the job that He was sent here to earth to accomplish. Now He sits at the right hand of our Father. If Jesus has finished our faith, then we should not have to ask anything more of Him. Everything else needing to be accomplished with our faith is up to us.

Always keep in mind that everyone was given a sufficient measure of faith needed to move mountains or to take care of the biggest or smallest of our problems. The key to using faith affectively is not to give up because you tried and it did not work the first time. If we treated everything else in our lives the way we treat faith, nothing would have ever been accomplished. We would have quit walking as a baby the first time we fell. We would have never learned to talk, much less go to school, get a job, or drive a car. We would have given up on everything in our life, but we did not give up on the important things in our lives. Never give up on faith. It is one of the most important things you will ever do in your life.

A child of God is tenacious, headstrong, and determined. You will never find an example in scripture of a defeated apostle. Keep pushing at that particular problem that is holding you back until it moves just a little. Because if you can move it just a little, your faith muscle is getting stronger and it will not be very long before the problem is completely out of your way and cast into the sea.

Jesus left you in charge of this world as His apostle. That includes being in charge of not only your life, but the world around you. You need to choose every day how you are going to work your faith muscle—or you will choose not to work your faith muscle at all.

Matthew 9:29 states, "According to your faith let it be to you." In scripture, Jesus is always attributing healing to the faith of the person being healed. Faith has always worked the same way. There is nothing new in the power and application of faith. It works the same way now as it did 2,000 years ago. It is about you and your knowledge and belief.

Is your faith working the way God intended for His gift to work? If not, you have something that you need to do. Open the gifts of your Father. In them you will find a note that says, "Included is everything you will need to live a long and joyful life. For best results, some exercise is required. For further details and instructions, see my Word. Please feel free to contact me in person if you have any questions. I would love to see you and spend the day with you."

The most important thing to remember about faith is never give up, never give in, and never use the world as a gauge to see how strong or weak your faith muscles are. Always use the promises of your Father as the only rule of faith. And after your faith has gotten stronger, teach your family, friends, and your neighbors how to work their faith muscle so that they too might take advantage of this wonderful gift of our Father. "Freely you were given, freely give."

17

Quantum Physics and Faith

There is far more evidence of the gifts of your Father in the scientific world than is realized by either science or the church. One of the wrong teachings of the Catholic Church was, and still is, that science and God must be separated. This was evident in the persecution demonstrated toward the scientific community because of discoveries that did not coincide with what the church believes to be real. It is not that all science has been correct through the ages. Or that even now it is 100 percent correct in its thinking today. However, the intricate workings of the world have existed since it was created. But because of the lack of understanding or the lack of technology, they were ignored or denied. Every day science is proving that what we, as God's children, called faith and belief play a much-bigger role in shaping the life of the individual and the influence we have on the entire world around us.

There are worlds within this world that we live in. There are other worlds that we do not see, such as the microscopic world, the cellular world, the atomic world, and the molecular world. These worlds within our world have always existed. But because man could not see or touch these worlds, he emphatically denied their existence until they were proven.

Every Christian in the world would agree that Jesus used power to accomplish the miracles that are talked about in scripture. Some Christians will even admit that the first-century church used the same power as Jesus did. However, very few Christians will admit that the same power that Jesus and the first-century apostles used is alive and with us today. And even fewer Christians will admit that they believe that all of creation was made with the same power that we are expected to utilize in our everyday lives.

Most Christians feel that it is blasphemy to say that we have God's own power at our disposal to use and utilize just as He did in the creation of the world, just as Jesus did in His ministry here on earth. Religion has always had a problem accepting the fact that the world could work in a different way, other than the way they have always perceived it.

An important aspect that needs to be understood by God's children is that if we are, in fact, working in that divine power, it is still a gift from our Father who created everything. This includes everything we see and everything we understand. This also includes everything we do not see and everything we do not understand.

Colossians 1:15–16 states, "He is the image of the invisible God, the first-born over all creation. For by Him all things were created that are in heaven and that are on earth, visible and invisible, whether thrones or dominions or principalities or powers. All things were created through Him and for Him." This verse says a great deal about what we already believe when it says that "God is invisible." Every Christian believes that there is a God and that you cannot see Him. But in most instances, this would be as far as they are willing to believe the invisible world exists. But the rest of this verse plainly tells us that He created not only a world that we see, but also the worlds we do not see.

We should never consider it blasphemy to try to understand this world or any of the invisible worlds. A big part of working in all the gifts and powers that your Father has provided for us is getting away from the basic ideas (wisdom) and principles of the world and what they believe to be real. Colossians 2:20 says, "Therefore, if you died with Christ from the basic principles of the world, why, as though living in the world, do you subject yourselves to regulations—"

We are not to regulate ourselves according to what the world believed to be right or wrong, actual or fantasy. We are, however, required to renew our minds according to the teachings of our Lord Jesus. Colossians 3:10 exhorts us, "and have put on the new man who is renewed in knowledge according to the image of Him who created him." The general idea about salvation and the workings of the gifts of our Father is through the understanding given to us by acquired information and knowledge.

Jesus walked on water, turn water into wine, fed thousands of people with a few fish and some bread. He changed the physical world around Him without using any physical laws that we are aware of. However, man is utilizing the law of gravity and always has been, without any understanding of why it works. Just because we do not understand the laws of physics does not mean that they are not available to us.

However, the science of quantum physics is beginning to prove that the world around us works through faith and belief. These realities have always been here. But we are just now beginning to understand how what we think and say will determine a change in the physical world.

The scientists who study quantum physics have made unbelievable breakthroughs recently in understanding the way the world actually works. For example, in his book *Message from Water*, Dr. Masaru Emoto explains his experiments on the molecular structure of water and what affects it. Dr. Emoto used water in his experiments because water is the most receptive of the four elements.

In his experiment, he exposed water to nonphysical elements. He applied mental stimuli in his study of the water and photographed it with a dark field microscope. And with this microscope he took pictures of the water from the Fujiwara Dam. Two types of pictures were taken of the water, water taken directly from the dam, and water taken from the dam that had been blessed by Zen Buddhist monks. The difference in the two pictures taken of the water are the difference between chaos and peace. The water that failed to receive the blessing was without a recognizable form or particular shape. The blessed water was quite the contrary. It resembled a perfectly shaped symmetrical snowflake. It was absolute proof that the molecules in the water could be changed by nothing more than the spoken word or belief.

Then Dr. Emoto took bottles of distilled water and taped words to the outside of the bottles. He then left these bottles out overnight. And using the same method of microscopic photography, took pictures of the water in these bottles the next day. In every case, there was an extreme difference in the makeup of the water molecules. When the words "love," "thank you," and other positive words were used, the same evidence of beauty and order were visible in the molecules of the water. When he used negative words, such as, "you make me sick," "I will kill you," and other words of a negative nature, the opposite and adverse reaction was evident in the water molecules. There was a noticeable chaotic and unorganized shape of the water molecule. Why this happens to the molecules of the water is unknown to the scientific community.

What is important to the children of God about these particular facts? Our body is made up of 90 percent water, and the world around us is made up of over 70 percent water. If our thoughts and words have a drastic effect on water, imagine what our thoughts and beliefs are doing to our bodies and the world around us.

Most people do not affect reality on a consistent substantial basis because they do not really believe in anything. And if they do affect the world, it is usually because of the negativity projected in their words and beliefs. Jesus told His disciples that if they would believe and not doubt that they could move a mountain. Religious teachings have reduced what Jesus was trying to explain by saying that the mountain is just any problem in your life. Jesus was, in fact, telling His disciples (including us) that the key to working the power from God and the unseen world was in believing you have the ability to do it. If you believe that you can make a physical change in the world, then the physical world around you will conform to that belief. This is the teaching that was consistent with everything that Jesus did.

Jesus always did things that defied the laws of physics. He learned how to do these things from the Father Himself. He explains in scripture that He only does what He sees the Father do. God spoke the Word, and by that Word things were created from nothing. Jesus believed it, and it was created from nothing. We are told in every part of the New Testament of the Bible to act like Jesus and to follow His example while He was here on earth. Why do we back up when it comes to working in the same power as He did? Because this would entail that we take responsibility to shape not only our own lives, but also to take responsibility for the shape that the world is in. If we, as God's children, accept the power to change the world, we would, in turn, have to accept the responsibility and the condition of that world. We would be required to get up every day, knowing that if our lives were good or bad, that the responsibility was only ours.

Hebrews 11:1 and 3 state, "Now faith is the substance [realization] of things hoped for, the evidence of things not seen… By faith we understand that the worlds were framed by the word of God, so that the things which are seen were not made of things which are visible." By these verses we are to understand that faith is something you cannot feel or touch, but becomes real through the evidence of a physical manifestation of what we are hoping for. This happens the same way that God created the world.

Things which we see in the world were not made as the world understands them. They were made from an unseen world, a world that only now science is beginning to reveal to God's children, so that the workings of faith might be demonstrated once again for the glory of our Father through His children.

We have become a people requiring proof for everything in our lives. God has chosen to reveal this mystery to us for this reason. Romans 16:25–26 says, "Now to him who is able to establish you according to my gospel and the preaching of Jesus Christ, according to the revelation of the mystery kept secret since the world began but now made manifest, and by the prophetic Scriptures made known to all nations, according to the commandment of the everlasting God, for obedience to the faith—"

First Corinthians 2:10 states, "But God has revealed them to us through His Spirit. For the Spirit searches all things, yes, the deep things of God." God's children were meant to work in His power. But it never says in scripture that this power ended with the death of the original 12 disciples. The power of God has never quit working from the time of creation, when He used it to create everything that we see and feel on this earth. The power has always been the same. We can still do everything that Jesus and His original 12 disciples could do. Jesus even tells us that we will do greater things than we have seen Him do.

This was one of the last teachings that He gave us before He went to sit at the right hand of our Father.

I am sorry to say that science is obtaining a greater knowledge of faith and how the power of God works than God's children. In the summer of 1993, 4,000 volunteers from hundred countries emerged on Washington, D.C. Their goal was to collectively meditate over a long period those days in order to change the crime rate of that city. It was predicted in advance that with the size of the group and the knowledge of past experiments, there would be a 25 percent drop in violent crimes as defined by the FBI in Washington that same year. The chief of police went on television and made a statement that "It would take 2 feet of snow to accomplish this claim." However, before the experiment was completed, the chief required his department to become collaborators with this group. Because, in fact, that summer, in the city of Washington, D.C., there was a 25 percent drop in violent crimes.

This was not the first time that an experiment of this nature was to take place. They obtained the expected results of 25 percent as compared to 48 previous studies and their outcomes.

I know what you are thinking to yourself, the scientists are not even Christians. How can they be working in God's power? First of all, not everyone mentioned in scripture who worked in God's power was a child of God. All through scripture there is an indication that a similar power was being used on the darker side. There has always been a power used on this earth. The rain falls on the just and the unjust alike. Everything in the world works the same for every person, with the exception of salvation. It works through understanding and belief in Jesus. For example, a law of gravity does not work only for God's children. Otherwise, anyone who was not a child of God would simply float away from the earth into space. The same is true with all of the other unseen mysteries of the natural laws of God.

Scripture tells us in many places that ungodly people worked in these laws throughout time. However, God's children always prevail in a battle of the use of these laws or powers. The reason for this is a person cannot work in this power for very long without the realization of who the Father is and the need for a Savior, Jesus. To put it simply, when you use this power, it has the same effect as all the gifts of our Father. It cannot help but bring you into an understanding of how wonderful your Father is. And by this understanding, cause you to establish a relationship with Him. And with this great knowledge and power together, nothing will be impossible for you, a child of God. To put it another way, it just works better with love.

I wrote this chapter with the intent of giving you a new outlook on the workings of faith through science. Never be afraid of science. You are a child of God, and if science can prove the workings of God's gifts to you, this can only serve to help your faith. It can only serve for the good of spreading the Gospel. Jesus used all of these unseen powers and told His disciples to go and do the same. You are God's child and a disciple of Jesus, with all the rights, privileges, and duties assigned to that station. Do not take my word for the truth. There is so much more about how quantum physics and your Father's gifts go hand-in-hand than I am able to compact into this chapter. You do not need to know how the television works in order to watch your favorite show; you simply need to know how to turn it on.

18
Why Fight? You Won!

Contrary to popular belief, the devil has been stripped of all his power and authority. I have tried to explain through the course of this book that you have more responsibility to the outcome of your life and the shape of this world than many of God's children have realized or have admitted to themselves. Along with the realization of who you are in God's plan comes the realization that the devil does not, and cannot, make you do anything in your life that you did not want to do in the first place.

Satan and his followers have been defeated, and then Jesus paraded them around for the whole world to see that they were beaten. Colossians 2:15 informs us, "Having disarmed principalities and powers, He made a public spectacle of them, triumphing over them in it."

First John 3:8 says, "He who sins is of the devil, for the devil has sinned from the beginning. For this purpose the Son of God was manifested, that He might destroy the works of the devil." If Jesus came to earth and did what God our Father asked Him to do, then the devil and his works are destroyed. Jesus did, in fact, come to earth, and made the statement that His work was finished, so unless Jesus is a liar and a slacker, the devil and any power that he may have had previously are now defeated.

First Peter 3:21–22 says, "There is also an antitype which now saves us— baptism (not the removal of the filth of the flesh, but the answer of a good conscience toward God), through the resurrection of Jesus Christ, who has gone into heaven and is at the right hand of God, angels and authorities and powers have been made subject to Him."

One more important point about the wonderful job that Jesus did when He finished the work of our Father is the fact of who He left in charge when He went to be with the Father. You guessed it. He left *us* in charge. He did not give the world back to Satan as the majority of the religious community would have you to believe.

Matthew 16:18–19 clearly says, "And I also say to you that you are Peter, and on this rock I will build My church, and the gates of Hades shall not prevail against it. And I will give you the keys of the kingdom of heaven, and whatever you bind on earth will be bound in heaven, and whatever you loose on earth will be loosed in heaven."

If you work for a large company and attained a position of authority and your superior handed you a set of keys to the business in question, what would this mean to you? It would mean that you have control over what happens in that business. It is exactly the same when Jesus gave the keys to us. We were to run the world and take care of it the way that Jesus taught us to. We are not doing a very good job, mainly because of our misconception brought on by religion. Because if we had continued in the direction that Peter and the first-century church was headed, the world would be a completely different place today. God's children continually give their power and authority away to an undeserving faction on a daily basis.

Every time that a story is told in scripture concerning Jesus and Satan, or one of Satan's followers, the venue is this. Jesus enters the scene and Satan or one of his demons immediately recognizes Jesus for who He is. They immediately start begging and pleading with Jesus to spare them. More times than not, they fall on their knees to present this plea.

I am not sure how you perceive these particular verses, but as for me, our adversary does not sound like he is much good in a fight whenever he comes against Jesus. Remember, we proved that Jesus dwells in us. So any enemy that Jesus has defeated we also have defeated.

Therefore, why do we always claim to be at war with the devil? Because we do not understand who we are or who Satan is. We do not even need to fight the devil; we just need to resist the devil. James 4:7 exhorts us, "Therefore submit to God. Resist the devil and he will flee from you."

First Peter 5:9 says, "Resist him, steadfast in the faith." It does not say in scripture that if you resist the devil that he will come against you even stronger. It says that if you resist the devil, he will flee from you. When something is fleeing it is trying to get away. How do we resist the devil? By submitting ourselves to God. How do we submit ourselves to God? Through the knowledge and understanding of who the Father is and what He has accomplished through the finished work of our Lord Jesus.

Romans 6:11 states, "Likewise you also, reckon [consider it so] yourselves to be dead indeed to sin, but alive to God in Christ Jesus our Lord." Never give the devil more credit than he deserves, and he deserves no credit. He is one of the dumbest creatures God ever made. He already had the relationship with God the Father that we as His children aspire to attain our whole lives. He has seen the face of God. He has seen God's power and glory. He has basked in the warmth of God's love. And because of his childish vanity, he has put himself in opposition to God. Now, I ask you, does this sound like an intelligent being to you?

In the scheme of the world and of your life, Satan is no more than an inconvenience, similar to the sugar ant that plagues your kitchen when you leave something sweet lying around on the countertop. If you stand and shout at (rebuke) the ants, you give them undue power in your life. But if you fix the problem, you will never even think of those sugar ants again, except to tell your friends of the problem and explain how you fixed it.

Never rebuke the devil unless you understand that it is for your own peace of mind. Note that it is not necessary to rebuke, just resist. You resist through knowledge, the knowledge that everything that could have been done to you, by the devil, was overcome by Jesus. Paul tells us in Ephesians 6 many things about who we fight and how to fight him. We fight against the wiles of the devil. If you break down what the "wiles of the devil" means, you will find that it simply means the scheming of the devil. It does not mean that you are being attacked by the devil. He is trying to trick you into hurting yourself through lies and schemes. He cannot do anything but lie and scheme, because he is defeated. Remember he has no power because of all that Jesus did with His finished work.

Paul continues to tell us that in order to withstand the scheming of the devil we need to put on the whole armor of God. It says in verse 6:14 to start with the truth. And the truth is only found in God's Word. If you know what God's Word says, then you have the truth. When it says to put on your "breastplate of righteousness," you need to bring to mind that it is God's righteousness that protects your heart. Know that His righteousness is more than sufficient to protect you from the damaging words, ideas, and worldly knowledge set forth by the devil.

Paul further explains in verse 15 that you need a good footing so that you do not trip and fall. This footing is attained through the knowledge of the Gospel (the Good News) that there is always peace between you and your Father. And there is nothing you can do to change the way God loves you. Nothing that you do good or bad will ever change that perfect love of your Father toward you. Always understand that you are righteous only because of Him and the work of our Lord Jesus.

Verse 16 tells us all about how to use the shield of faith. Faith, or belief, is the power given to you by your Father to determine the outcome of your world. And when you use faith or belief to make the change in your world, you become a witness that everything that Satan has said to you previously is now proven to be a lie. The more you work in the power of faith, the more the devil sounds like a gnat in your ear. He has no more power or validity to change your life than that gnat.

And in verse 17, Paul tells us to put on the helmet, the helmet of salvation. The helmet guards the head; it guards your mind against everything that is not the Word of God. Discern this Word with the sword of the Spirit (God's Spirit that lives in you). And the Word of God tells you that you believe, and therefore, your salvation is secured.

Traditionally, the sword was viewed as a weapon that we would use to kill Satan. But if you look at Hebrews 4:12, it clearly states, "For the word of God is living and powerful, and sharper than any two-edged sword, piercing even to the division of soul and spirit, and of joints and marrow, and is a discerner of the thoughts and intents of the heart." The sword of our Father (the Word of God) is what we use on our own thoughts and intents to keep ourselves from being deceived by Satan. The devil has nothing to come at you with except lies and deception. And if you believe any of what I have explained in this book, you will not only be able to resist the devil, you will not even give him another thought.

The devil has no more power in your life than a door-to-door salesman. And oddly enough, he uses some of the same tactics. He will present to you something that is lacking in your life that oftentimes we did not even know we needed. Then he will present this something in a way that you do not know how you lived without it. He will make this something sound so wonderful, that you will convince yourself that you must have it. And as in the sales world, it usually sounds better than it is. But it never works the way that it should work. And the cost is always higher than expected.

I am not saying that you do not have a legitimate need for this something. What I am saying is that cannot be filled by the devil.

Another similarity between the devil and a door-to-door salesman is that the company will choose people who believe in the product to go door-to-door to sell that product. The devil also uses people to try to sell you a wrong thought or idea. Second Thessalonians 3:2–3 says, "and that we may be delivered from unreasonable and wicked men; for not all have faith. But the Lord is faithful, who will establish you and guard you from the evil one."

It is through a lack of faith and trust in God and the knowledge of the finished work of Jesus that we can be convinced of something that is untrue. Do not believe anyone that states something contrary to what you know to be your Father's nature and His will for His children. Do not listen to the sales pitch when you know that God's Word says just the opposite. If it is because of a sales pitch that Satan has presented to you that you suddenly noticed a lack in your life, go and talk to your Father, and your need will be filled. Or you can open and use one of the many gifts that your Father has provided for that very purpose.

Know in your heart, without a doubt, that whatever you buy from the sales pitch of Satan, the cost is too great and the product is obviously inferior to what you already possess. Weigh your needs and wants on the scale of godly wisdom and you will find that many things that you thought were a need in your life are really no more than just a want. But because of a good sales pitch, you really believe that you could not live without it.

The good news about this idea of being deceived by the sales pitch of Satan is when you buy into it, it is just more junk that you have to get rid of and that is all that it is. But if you learn to recognize the scheming of the devil, you will not buy into his lies. If you would not have listened to his sales pitch in the beginning, if you would have recognized who he was in the first place, you would have never been sold an inferior product with the claim that it is as good as the real thing.

When you have used and utilized everything that your Father has given you, it is easy to tell the difference between God's gifts and the knockoff that Satan offers. When you hold the love of your Father up against the love of the world, the contrast is the difference between light and dark. The only legitimate free gift ever offered in this world is a free gift from our Father. Every other free gift offered by the world has an exorbitant cost connected to some outlandish sales pitch. Always look for the cost and be a smart consumer where your spiritual life is concerned. After all, it does not take a financial genius to decide that free is better.

19
Why Not Open
Your Gifts Today?

I hope that while you have been reading this book that you might have come to the realization that everything that you need for both your spiritual walk and your walk here on earth stem from your relationship with your Father in heaven. It has been this way since the beginning of man's creation. If you are lacking the kind of one-on-one personal relationship that you desire with your Father, why not start today? By seeking your Father and establishing just such a relationship, then there is no reason that your new and wonderful life would not also begin today.

Remember to always look at the new covenant of peace when you are looking at a description of the law in scripture. And that even in the name "New Gospel of peace" is the description of its meaning. Because of that covenant, we have a contract from God of everlasting peace. God your Father is never mad at you. Even if you feel in your heart that you have broken this contract, this has nothing to do with God. It is just your feelings, emotions, and misunderstandings that are making you feel that way because God does not feel the same way about what you have done or have not done, as you do. He made a promise never to be mad at you or anyone ever again. If you doubt this fact, always look into the perfect love of God for the answers. And from this vantage point, you will always see God's nature, His sacrifice, and His forgiveness. And with this knowledge of who your Father is, combined with who you are because of the finished work of Jesus, you will always run to your Father and never run away from Him, even when you feel that you have done something wrong. You will always go to Him out of love, not fear.

If you feel a need to obey any certain law or doctrine, then obey the laws and doctrines that we are instructed to obey, such as the law and doctrine of godly love brought to us from God, by Jesus. You must learn to love the way that Jesus taught us to love, the way Jesus loves our Father and every one of His children. We must stop trying to love the way the world loves. Godly love is perpetual, and if you start every day with the intention of love for your Father and His children, before very long, you won't even remember when you did not love in this manner. Do not get caught up in the net of religion, with its Old Testament covenant of rules and regulations. Live a life of love, the kind of love that the Lord Jesus teaches us through His example of how He lived and loved.

I am sure that as you were reading this book, many things in it were contrary to your previous teachings, beliefs, and even your nature in general. When I first realized the real truth, it went against my worldly nature also. But after the man-made lies had all been disproved, I had no other choice than to accept the love and peace that comes from this realization. I understood that it was because of my inability to let go of my old teachings of the world, and the old man and his misunderstandings of doctrines of religion, that I was bound by the shackles of religious misconceptions. But my primary problem was that my old, earth-born man was reluctant to give way to my new, godly man because of guilt and self-condemnation. I had a hard time realizing the fact that I had to accept all the gifts from my Father and that I had to let go of the world and its corrupt ideas in order to embrace the new nature, the new man or woman.

You must realize that it is not your old nature you are trying to rebuild or remodel. Your old nature must be torn to the ground, and Jesus, and God's nature put in its place. And with this mind-set there will be little or no trace of your old nature or your old man or woman. But first, as Jesus said, in order to start a new life, you must "be reborn."

If on the completion of this book you realize how special you are in the world and in the eyes of our Father, then this book has been a success. You should realize that you are an adopted child of the only God, and with that choice that God made to bring you into His family, He also chose to provide you with every gift that you would ever need, in eternity and for your life here on earth. That with this adoption you were made equal heirs with His only begotten Son, our Savior Jesus Christ, because now with the adoption, you have the stature, rights, and privileges of a child of God. The only requirement that you have in order to take advantage of these gifts is just to accept them and believe in the Father and His Son who provided them. Salvation and every good gift from the Father were yours the second the adoption was final.

God's Word is everything today and tomorrow that it was when He spoke it yesterday. God's Word has not lost its power or potency over time. It is as strong today as when the patriarchs used it. It is as vital, and as valid, as it was when Jesus and His first disciples used it so eloquently. Put your faith in the Word of your Father, and know that His Word is always true. By using His Word, you have the ability to judge everything in this world and in heaven. His Word will guard and protect your heart. But if you do not know and understand His Word, it can do none of these things for you. Know your Father's nature and His Word. Through the knowledge of God's nature, His Word will reveal the truth. And through that nature and the power of His Word, your walk and your relationship will know no bounds.

Do not sit and wait for a sign from your Father. You hold in your hand a book of letters detailing the nature of your Father and every instruction that He has for His children. His Word will inform you of who you are, where you come from, and where you are going. And even more important than any of these is the fact that His Word tells you that you are never alone in this world. It tells you that you are always loved by the Creator of this world. It tells you that because of these facts, you should never be afraid. It tells you that your Father has already anticipated every contingency in your life and has provided you with every gift that you would need to rectify any problem that you might face. Because with these concerns out of your everyday life, you will have more time for a loving relationship with your Father, with your Savior Jesus Christ, and every one of God's children that you come in contact with.

Knowledge is great, but belief is greater. Always test your knowledge before you allow it to become belief, because what you truly believe will determine what manifests in your life. Believe what the Word of God tells you. Believe in the teachings of our Lord Jesus. Believe in yourself as an adopted child of the only God. Believe that you could do nothing to attain this place in God's family on your own ability. Nothing is impossible for you because of all the gifts from your Father and His ability in you to accomplish what the world would believe is impossible. Believe that it is always His ability that now works in you and allows you to accomplish such great things. Believe that His nature toward His children is always a nature of love and forgiveness. And when you believe all of these things, the mountains that you encounter through your life, no matter how big or how small, will simply throw themselves into the sea. It is about what you believe, not what you know.

Always remain cognizant of the fact that you must guard your heart. You must never allow anything to enter into your heart that has not been approved by your mind and your spirit. Filter everything that tries to enter your heart through your thoughts and your emotions through the Spirit of God. Filter all knowledge through the nature of your Father, His Word, and the teachings of Jesus. Never allow something into your heart because of a falsely elevated station of an individual or organization. View everything in this world through the gifts that were provided by your Father.

His Spirit lives in you. Simply ask Him for help in determining what should be allowed in your heart and what should not be allowed. But this requires something on your part in order for this to work correctly. After you ask God's Spirit, you need to be quiet and listen to what the answer is. If what is being written on your heart does not comply with love, forgiveness, peace, and joy, then you might take another look at the information and refuse to write it on your heart.

The law is law; it does not matter if it is the Law of Moses or the law of a church disguised as a doctrine, even if it was created with the intention to help

God control His children. It is still a law, and you made the choice not to live by the law any longer. If I have failed to explain this fact, please continue to read God's Word until you prove it to yourself. You cannot live by the righteousness of God and the law simultaneously. You must choose to live by one or the other. You chose righteousness when you chose Jesus. Let go of the law—any law—and live with the freedom that comes from that release.

One of the most wonderful and precious gifts that God provided for His children is His righteousness. Not just any righteousness but the righteousness of God Himself. He took His own righteousness and gave it to each one of His adopted children. And the reason that this gift is so important is that we could never have had a relationship with our Father without His righteousness. But because of this gift of righteousness, we are righteous and fulfill every requirement needed to move ahead toward salvation and a wonderful life with our Father. On our own we could never have hoped to attain even a glimpse of righteousness, but because of the finished work of Jesus and the Good News that lies in that finished work, we are able to be adopted into God's family, never again to be on our own. Our Father is always there with another gift to help us with our every need.

You are the Creator's son or daughter. Do not try to become something before you accept this fact. People will tell you that because of sin you cannot be a prince or princess of the Most High King. They would tell you to go and try to do better, and maybe later you can be exalted into that position of God's child. Maybe if you give enough, pray enough, fast enough, or go to church an indeterminate number of years, you might acquire the status of a son or daughter of God. Never believe these lies! You are everything you need to be *right now* because of God your Heavenly Father and Jesus your Savior. Never look at you and see yourself. Always look at you and see God's child.

The Gospel is always the Good News about the relationship between you and God. What Jesus has done that He has corrected all sin and unrighteousness. Anytime that you hear something other than the Good News being taught as the Gospel of peace, it is a false doctrine initiated by man. If, when you are sitting in church or Sunday school, or listening to the radio or television, and you hear a message of judgment, condemnation, or any works to attain righteousness, you simply need to turn off the radio or television, or get up and run; do not walk to the nearest exit. This kind of teaching will only do damage to your heart and life. Recognize what the true Gospel of peace entails. Always realize that with this new covenant, God has only love and forgiveness for His children.

Learn what God's Word really says so that the deception of thousands of false doctrines will have no effect on your life or your relationship with your Father. The only breach that can exist between you and your Father is in your mind if you take the teaching of a false doctrine into your heart. Then, you cause a separation between you and your Father because of a wrong belief. You would do just like Adam did in the Garden. Because of misinformation, you will feel that God is mad at you, and therefore, you will run away from Him when you should be running to Him.

Question the status quo of any teaching. It does not matter how long a teaching has been established as a particular doctrine. This only means that they have been teaching a wrong message for a longer period of time. And because of this wrong doctrine, there is a multitude of wrong teachings written on the hearts of God's children. And because their hearts received the wrong information, they are unable to lie down in the peace, freedom, and the rest that Jesus died to provide for them.

Examine all of scripture as a whole. Never take a verse out of context. Look for the word or words that totally change the meaning of a particular idea or thought. Examine scripture with the intent of putting it back in line with the nature of your Father and the finished work of Jesus Christ. If scripture does not line up with the truth of who your Father is, who Jesus is and what His finished work has accomplished for His children, then keep looking until you find the truth. Scripture must line up with the nature of God, or everything that we have been told by God and His Son would be a lie. And because we know that God and Jesus cannot lie, then there must be a misinterpretation in the Word if it shows anything but their nature in the interpretation. Look for the "ifs," "ands," or "buts" in scripture and you will always come to realize the truth.

If you rely on your own ability, my friend, you will always fall short of your own expectations. For this reason, we were given God's grace. If you recall from the previous chapter on grace, the definition is God's ability to work in your heart to affect a change in your life. One more time, you have to realize that you can do nothing on your own to change your life apart from the acceptance of the gifts from your Father, one of these gifts being the ability to become the new man or woman that you need to become. You are not a sinner saved by grace. You are a righteous child of God if you received God's ability and righteousness to perfect the change in your life. You are no longer a sinner. If you believe anything else, it is from the teachings of doctrines of men and not of scripture.

You are born with all the faith you need to do every great work you have ever heard about. You cannot obtain more faith than you already have. But you can work your faith muscle until you have accomplished the things that up until now you thought were impossible or not for someone like you. When you work your faith muscle and do not give up, your faith will get stronger, and when faith gets stronger, you will get more done, and when you get more done, your faith will get stronger. Try to lift a little over and over with your faith muscle. And before long, you will be lifting more and more, and bigger and bigger things until you will not even remember not having such a strong faith muscle as you do now. It is like every other muscle that you have in your body. If it goes unused it becomes weak. But if you use it every day, it cannot help but become stronger. And also like every other muscle in your body, there is no end to how strong you can become if you continue to exercise.

Science and faith go hand in hand. Look into some of the things that quantum physics have proven about our thoughts, emotions, and beliefs, and how they play a part in changing the physical world around us. If you will research some of the experiments that have been done by the scientific community, you will discover there is more to your makeup as a child of God than was previously thought possible. If you studied just a small portion of quantum physics science with an open mind, you will see that there is evidence of the workings of God's gifts. Expel the teaching that science and the church must remain separated in order to live a godly life. Understand that God gave His children a reasonable explanation for His gifts, and this is by no means blasphemy, nor does it take anything away from God's power. In fact, it only serves to further strengthen our case of a single Creator of all things, and that His creation works perfectly just the way He said it would. Realize that this creation was made for us; we were not made for this creation.

Our Father gave Jesus a job to do. Jesus, in turn, gave us a job to do. God never expected His children to do what He asked of them without giving them the proper tools to complete that task. He has given us everything that we need to complete every good work of His will. Nothing can stop you from accomplishing everything that scripture says you are capable of doing. Accept your own belief. Not even the devil has any power over your life or your walk with God that you do not give to him. Satan is the reason that Jesus came to the earth. And when Jesus came to the earth, one of His primary goals was to defeat the devil. And He did exactly that; He defeated the devil.

Never give Satan more authority, power, or credit than is due him. He is nothing but a nuisance to the world, and because of Jesus' death, burial, and resurrection, Satan is a defeated adversary. The only people that are still at war with the devil are people that did not hear or understand that the war is over, that Satan was defeated. Treat him as the nuisance he is. It is not necessary to fight him; it is only necessary to resist him. Why fight when you have already won?

I hope that you have enjoyed this book. But more than that, I hope that this book made you think about who your Father really is, what His nature has always been, and what it is now. And what your relationship with your Father is because of what He did through Jesus.

I hope whether the revelation came to you like a flash of fire or has gradually entered into your heart, that you have come to the realization that it is not about your limited abilities as a man, but with the supernatural abilities of God that you will substantiate a change in your life, and, in turn, continually change the world around you to conform to an image of heaven.

First John 4:4 tells us, "You are of God, little children, and have overcome them, because He who is in you is greater than he who is in the world." Always remember who you are and why you are able to do the things you do. Never hesitate any time, day or night, for the rest of your life, to crawl up in your Heavenly Father's lap, thank Him, and tell Him how much you love Him, and let Him love you in return like only He can.

It is my prayer that you would take what you have learned in this book and you will put it into practice in your everyday life, and I hope that you will start today.

Sources

All scripture quotations are from The Holy Bible, New King James Version, copyright 1982, by Thomas Nelson Inc.

All Greek and Hebrew definitions and translations are from *The New Strong's Exhaustive Concordance of the Bible*, copyright 1990, by Thomas Nelson Publishing and Vine, W. E. (William Edwy), 1873–1949 (complete expository dictionary with topical index), copyright 1984, 1996, Thomas Nelson Inc.

Chapter 17, "Quantum Physics of Faith," is from *What the Bleep Do We Know!?* copyright 2004, Twentieth Century Fox Home Entertainment Inc.

Dr. Masaru Emoto's *Messages from Water* and "A Study on Maharishi Effect" written by John Hagelin, Ph.D., professor of physics and director of the Institute of Science, Technology, and Public Policy at Maharishi University.

Copyright Registration Number TXu1-787-276

Effective Date of registration December 2, 2011

CPSIA information can be obtained
at www.ICGtesting.com
Printed in the USA
LVHW051628260621
691200LV00006B/83